Top 100
Low Fat Recipes

Top 100 Low Fat Recipes

Judith Wills

<u>headline</u>

This publication constitutes an exclusive abridgement of
Top 200 Low Fat Recipes by Judith Wills for *Top Santé* magazine.

The full edition is published by Headline Book Publishing, priced £18.99

First published in 2003
by HEADLINE BOOK PUBLISHING

This edition produced specially for *Top Santé* in 2004

10 9 8 7 6 5 4 3 2 1

ISBN 0 7553 1371 2

Set in Helvetica Neue
Designed by Isobel Gillan

Printed and bound in Great Britain by
Mackays of Chatham plc, Chatham, Kent

HEADLINE BOOK PUBLISHING
A division of Hodder Headline
338 Euston Road
London NW1 3BH

www.headline.co.uk
www.hodderheadline.com

contents

introduction

I love planning what to eat. I love cooking. I love eating. And most of all I love the fact that I can do all three without feeling guilty and without spoiling my waistline or damaging my health. The truth is that it isn't difficult to rustle up the most delicious snacks, lunches, salads, suppers, stews and even desserts which are both low in fat and low in calories. This book contains 100 examples to prove the point.

I have spent the past ten years or more testing, adapting and devising recipes which pass my 'taste test' and the other criteria for inclusion in this book – low fat, ease of preparation and, with a few exceptions, reasonable cost. I have also aimed to provide a balance of traditional, much-loved recipes, such as chilli con carne, coq au vin and pasta carbonara, in a reduced-fat, reduced-calorie format alongside less well-known or new dishes which are naturally light and delicious. On every page there are cooking, ingredient, shopping and preparation tips, and there are plenty of variations on the basic recipes as appropriate.

I don't believe that low-fat cooking means that you have to avoid using small amounts of good quality oils and so you may be surprised to find olive and a few other oils in many recipes, even butter now and then. My cooking is straightforward and easy with no complicated tricks to learn in order to avoid fat.

This chapter contains all you need to know about devising for yourself and your family, a healthy, weight-conscious diet. It also gives meal suggestions to suit all for every time of day, including breakfast.

I truly believe that the collection of recipes in this book is 'the best' and provides enough variety for anyone who wants to cook in a healthy but enjoyable way for years to come.

Happy cooking!

What makes a healthy low-fat diet?

Healthy eating is most certainly not about cutting all fat out of your diet, nor is it a simple matter of reducing calories. First and foremost, healthy eating is about getting enough of all the nutrients that your body needs for health – a balance of protein, carbohydrate, fibre, vitamins, minerals and even fats that we need for proper functioning. Yes, we all NEED fat.

So why a 'low-fat' cookbook? Simple – the recipes and meal suggestions will enable you to reduce fat levels to the internationally agreed acceptable amount of 25 per cent of the total calories in your diet, but, in doing so, they still incorporate enough of the 'healthy fats' that you really do need for good health.

Reduce fat sensibly

These 'healthy fats' are called omega-3 and omega-6, which are part of the polyunsaturated group of fats. In fact, most of us get plenty of omega-6 in our diets and so it is omega-3, which is present in greatest quantity in oily fish and also in some seeds, nuts and vegetables, of which we need to make an effort to eat more. These fats help to keep us healthy in many ways by protecting against heart disease, stroke and some cancers. They are also linked to protection against Alzheimer's disease, arthritis and skin complaints such as eczema, help to protect the immune and reproductive systems and are vital in pregnancy and for a healthy brain.

Another category of healthy fats are the monounsaturated fats, found in greatest quantities in olive oil, rapeseed oil, groundnut oil, avocados and many nuts. These fats are also important in helping to keep a healthy heart, blood cholesterol and blood lipids. I usually use them in cooking as they are more stable than some fats when heated.

The fats that you can cut back on without detriment to your health – and, indeed, reducing them is linked with protection against heart disease and weight problems – are the saturated fats. These fats are found in greatest quantities in full-fat dairy produce, such as full-cream milk, cream, hard and cream cheeses and butter, and also in fatty cuts of meat, such as shoulder of lamb, stewing beef, pork crackling, as well as in lard and in many commercially made products, including pastries, pies, cakes, biscuits, desserts and much more. These commercial products are also likely to contain undesirable levels of trans or hydrogenated fats – commercially hardened polyunsaturated fats.

Saturated fats and trans fats are those closely linked with the increased risk of heart disease, stroke and other circulatory diseases and, because they are often present in foods that are also high in sugar and/or calories, with obesity. Cut back on these foods and you can save hundreds of calories and many grams of fat a day without hunger and without pain.

Fat, slimming and weight control

Many of us want to cut back on fat because we believe it is an easy way to cut calories, as well as a healthier way to eat. Indeed, research shows that cutting down on the amount of fat that you eat is the simplest way to lose weight and the easiest way to stay slim long term.

The United States Department of Agriculture (USDA) states that people who cut fat – even while making no other changes to their diets – lose weight steadily, and that it is people who maintain a reduced-fat diet (and take regular exercise) who manage to keep the weight off.

introduction

The best type of low-fat diet to follow, the USDA and the World Health Organisation recommend, is not, however, an extremely low-fat diet (one that contains around 10–15 per cent of your daily calories as fat) but a moderately low-fat diet that contains around 25 per cent fat.

The 25 per cent level – achieved by cutting intake of saturated and trans fats, while retaining omega-3 and -6 in the diet – seems to be the one which provides a range of health benefits, while offering the most chance of success in weight control. This is partly because it is not unworkably low in fat. Very low-fat diets have what is termed 'low compliance', since people don't stick to them for long because they find them boring, restrictive and unpalatable. By the way, fat occurs naturally in a wide range of healthy foods (almost all foods, even green vegetables and grains, for instance) so the concept of a 'fat-free' diet is actually impossible unless you fast – another bad idea!

The recipes in this book, when eaten as part of a balanced meal with the suggested accompaniments as appropriate, will help you to keep to a 25 per cent fat diet, and restrict saturated fats but not the other healthier fats.

The chart opposite shows you how much fat you should aim to eat a day, both for weight control and for slimming, including my guidelines on how much of that fat you might eat at each meal. Remember it's all about balance – if you choose a higher-fat main meal, then pick a lower-fat lunch.

Keep it low every day

Obviously, the recipes in this book are all low in fat but when preparing breakfasts, snacks and other non-recipe lunches and main meals, you can easily keep fat down to healthy levels by using the following tips:

- Right now, go through your larder, chuck out old/stale/boring/high-fat items. Make a list and restock with plenty of low-fat, low-cal seasonings, canned tomatoes, pulses, pasta, wholegrains and other items using ideas from the checklist opposite.
- Invest in a few good quality cooking utensils (see ideas opposite) which will help you to reduce the amount of fat needed in cooking.
- Cheese lovers will be relieved to hear that a small amount of very strong cheese, such as real Parmesan, extra-mature farmhouse Cheddar or Gruyère, goes a long way in cooking and may in the end save you more fat and calories than a portion of a reduced-fat, mild cheese, while also being better for your psyche. Grating cheese also makes it go further.
- Always use a cooking oil spray (available in ready-to-use spray pump cans at the supermarket, or you can buy your own empty spray can and fill it according to the manufacturer's instructions) instead of pouring oil into the pan when frying and browning foods such as meat, bacon and poultry.
- Always buy the leaner cuts of meat, often labelled 'extra lean' or 'less than 10 per cent' or '5 per cent' fat. Some pundits will tell you that these lean cuts don't give enough flavour or moisture to a finished dish, or may be tough, but if you cook them correctly this needn't be the case, and I certainly don't find them so.
- Make full use of the naturally low-fat cooking methods, such as grilling, griddling, steaming, poaching, baking and cooking in parchment.

The amount of fat you need a day

	Typical adult female*	
	slimming diet (1,500 calories a day) 25% fat	weight maintenance diet (2,000 calories a day) 25% fat
Total grams of fat needed	**42g**	**56g**
*Sample breakdown***		
Breakfast	5g	5–8g
Lunch	12–15g	15–18g
Evening meal	17–20g	20–25g
Snacks/desserts	5g	5–10g

*Males should increase weight maintenance and slimming calories and fat by 25 per cent.
**For guidance only; the exact amount of fat that you eat at each meal isn't important as long as your overall daily fat intake is within the guidelines.

- Make full use of naturally low-fat meals, such as vegetable soups, white fish, pulses, pasta and other grains with vegetable sauces, salads with a simple low-fat dressing, sandwiches with low-fat fillings, such as turkey, lean ham, skinless chicken and plenty of salad.
- Include plenty of naturally tasty seasonings in your meals – fresh herbs, fresh and dried spices, vinegars, soy and Worcestershire sauce, citrus juices, mushroom ketchup, sun-dried vacuum-packed tomatoes, and so on. These will help to satisfy tastebuds, which are used to getting flavour from fat.
- Eat smaller portions of the higher-fat foods such as meat, moderate-fat cheese, full-fat yogurt and desserts, and larger portions of vegetables, salad, fruit and very low-fat protein foods like skimmed milk, low-fat yogurt and low-fat fromage frais. If your plate is full and looks attractive with plenty of colours and textures, you will not feel as if you are being deprived. But don't feel you have to give up these higher-fat foods completely – many of them offer a good range of nutrients, including calcium and protein in cheese, and iron and protein in red meat.
- For sandwiches and things on toast you can do without butter or other high-fat spreads. To prevent salad-filled sandwiches from going soggy, spread the bread very lightly with reduced-calorie mayonnaise (such as Hellmann's Light), which also adds taste and moisture.
- Aim for plenty of variety in your diet – boredom is a killer for a food lover, and can make you think you are hungry/crave a box of chocolates.
- Shop wisely, when you aren't hungry. What you don't buy, you can't eat.

Vegetarian recipes

Vegetarian recipes are indicated with a ⊗ symbol.

Kitchen utensils

You may already have all the utensils you need for low-fat cooking – check down this list to see what I consider almost essential (over and above the things you are bound to have, such as a few saucepans, stirring spoons and so on).

- A really good quality, heavy non-stick frying pan or even better, one large one and one small one.
- A casserole dish with a tight-fitting lid, preferably a flameproof one, which will save you a lot of bother when cooking stews, braises and casseroles.
- A really good quality, heavy baking tray for roasting vegetables, etc. A cheap thin one will tend to burn, not bake your food.
- A couple of heatproof, non-metal curved spatulas for sautéing and a couple of flat, heatproof, non-metal spatulas for turning food in your non-stick pan.

You might also like to consider a ridged cast iron griddle pan, a lifetime investment for the committed griller, and decent kitchen scales, which weigh in small increments of 2g. A lot of cheaper kitchen scales don't weigh less than 20g accurately, which is important for both calories and fats (if you are weighing out butter or cheese, for example) and for precision cooking, such as most baking and desserts.

Planning your low-fat diet

Whether you want to lose weight or simply cut down on the amount of fat you eat, the following suggestions will help you devise a diet that suits. Try to mix and match your meals so that you eat a wide variety of food types – if you have meat in the evening, have a vegetarian or fish lunch, for example. Drink plenty of water – aim for six glasses a day – and don't go overboard on high-caffeine drinks. Remember there are calories in most drinks; allow yourself a 200–250ml skimmed milk allowance a day for use in hot drinks or on its own.

For slimming

Select one of the following suggestions or the recipes in this book to give a maximum total fat intake of 42g a day. Try to ensure that your daily calorie total adds up to no more than 1,500 (for women) but no less than 1,250 (eat extra low-fat snacks if your chosen meals don't add up to at least this). Men can increase calorie and fat intake by 25 per cent for weight loss. Each day:

- choose from one of the following breakfasts (5g fat maximum)
- choose from one of the following snacks or a dessert (5g fat maximum)
- select a recipe lunch – a soup, snack or salad, for example (12–15g fat)
- select a recipe main meal – a quick hob supper, pasta, grill or stew, for example (17–20g fat).

Breakfasts *(maximum 250 calories; 5g fat)*

- 125ml pot low-fat natural bio yogurt with 25g muesli, 1 teaspoon linseeds and 1 chopped apple.
- 100g pot low-fat fruit diet fromage frais; 25g slice wholemeal bread with 1 teaspoon low-fat spread and 2 teaspoons low-sugar marmalade; 1 small banana.
- 5 tablespoons baked beans on 40g slice wholemeal bread; 1 glass orange juice.
- 2 Weetabix or 30g unsweetened breakfast cereal (not muesli) with 125ml skimmed milk; 25g slice wholemeal bread with 1 teaspoon low-fat spread and 1 teaspoon Marmite.

Snacks *(maximum 100 calories; 5g fat)*

- 100g pot low-fat fruit diet fromage frais; 1 satsuma, plum or kiwifruit.
- 2 dark rye crispbread topped with 1 tablespoon low-fat soft cheese, cherry tomatoes or apple slices.
- 25g slice wholemeal bread with 1 teaspoon low-fat spread and Marmite.
- 1 medium banana and 3 ready-to-eat dried apricots.

For weight maintenance

Select one of the following suggestions or the recipes in this book to give a maximum total fat intake of 56g a day. Try to ensure that your daily calorie total adds up to no more than 2,000 (for women), so if your chosen meals come to less than this eat extra low-fat snacks. Men can increase calorie and fat intake by 25 per cent. Each day:

- choose from one of the following breakfasts (maximum 8g fat)
- choose from one of the following snacks (maximum 10g fat)
- select a recipe lunch (15–18g fat)
- select a recipe main meal (20–25g fat).

Breakfasts *(maximum 350 calories; 8g fat)*

- 60g luxury muesli with 125ml skimmed milk, topped with 1 chopped apple and 1 segmented tangerine.
- 40g Fruit 'n Fibre with 125ml skimmed milk, topped with 100g berry fruits or 1 kiwifruit; 40g slice wholemeal bread with 1 teaspoon low-fat spread and 2 teaspoons low-sugar jam.
- 1 medium egg, boiled, with 40g slice wholemeal bread with 1 teaspoon low-fat spread; 1 medium banana; 100ml glass orange juice.
- 3 medium tomatoes, halved and fried in a non-stick pan with 1 teaspoon butter on 40g slice wholemeal toast; 125ml pot low-fat diet fruit yogurt.

Snacks *(maximum 200 calories; 10g fat)*

- 1 large plain digestive biscuit; 1 dessertspoon pumpkin seeds; 1 apple.
- Sandwich made with 2 × 25g slices wholemeal bread, filled with sliced tomato and 2 slices extra-lean ham; 1 orange.
- 150g pot low-fat rice pudding; 1 apple or pear.
- 300ml any New Covent Garden vegetable soup; 2 dark rye Ryvitas.
- Sandwich made with 2 × 25g slices brown bread, spread with low-fat mayonnaise and filled with 50g tuna in water or brine, well drained, and lettuce.

Dinner party menus

If you're planning a supper party for friends or family, balance your menu so that there is a complementary mix of flavours, ingredients and styles. Remember the following tips:

- Meals often work best when each course comes from a similar area of the world.
- If you're having meat for your main course, avoid a meat starter. The same applies to fish, chicken, cheese and pulses.
- If you have a soup starter, go for a 'dry' main course, while a 'dry' starter can be happily followed by a gravy-rich main course or casserole.
- You need have no more than one, or at most two, hot courses. In summer, they can all be cold.
- Don't have the same dominant flavour in more than one course – tomato sauce, for instance, or a strong herb such as basil or coriander.
- If one of your courses is relatively high in fat, pick a low-fat starter and dessert.
- Aim for no more than 30g fat per portion for a special occasion three-course meal, a figure which should fit in reasonably well with most people's low-fat diets – although it is possible to devise many three-course meals from the recipes in this book for much less than that.

snacks and starters

The recipes in this chapter can also be served as a light lunch or supper, or as a starter for a dinner party. Many of the soup recipes in the next chapter, the salad recipes on pages 102–10 and half portions of some of the pasta and grain recipes on pages 92–100 are also suitable as snacks or starters.

When choosing a starter for a three-course meal, aim to restrict the fat content to no more than 8g per portion – or another way to provide a healthy balanced meal is to aim for a maximum of 30g fat for the whole meal and pick your three courses from the various chapters in this book accordingly.

There are many other quick and easy ideas for snacks and starters that don't really need a recipe. Try griddled thinly sliced Mediterranean vegetables, such as aubergines or courgettes, drizzled with a little olive oil and balsamic vinegar, for example, or roasted asparagus or baby vine tomatoes with a vinaigrette or a squeeze of lemon juice and black pepper.

Fruits, of course, are an ideal low-fat and low-calorie starter. You need not feel guilty about serving a simple ripe, juicy, orange-fleshed melon or plump fresh figs, or try sprinkling red grapefruit segments with sugar, grill them and serve with a green salad.

You could serve a selection of vegetable crudités, such as carrot, celery, onion and chicory, with a simple tzatziki-type dip of Greek yogurt, garlic and cucumber with seasoning. For a spicy dip, mix the yogurt with a little tomato sauce and finely chopped chilli.

If your main meal is one of the heartier, higher-calorie selections in this book, no one will want a substantial starter, so don't be afraid to serve just a well-dressed green salad.

melon, prosciutto and ginger salad

Serves 4 | 60 calories per portion | 3g fat per portion

70g pack prosciutto (Parma ham)

cooking oil spray (optional)

1 ripe Cantaloupe melon, sliced into wedges and peeled, reserving any juice

1 dsp balsamic vinegar

1.5cm piece of fresh root ginger, very finely grated

fresh mint leaves, to garnish

1 Preheat the grill to medium. Grill the prosciutto, or spray a non-stick frying pan with a little cooking oil and fry until crisp. Allow to cool a little, then roughly crumble and set aside.

2 Arrange the melon slices on four serving plates and scatter the prosciutto on top.

3 Combine any juices from the melon with the balsamic vinegar and the ginger, mixing well (see Tip). Drizzle the dressing over the melon and garnish with mint leaves.

tip If your melon doesn't yield much juice, add 1 tablespoon of orange or apple juice to the vinegar and ginger mixture.

antipasto

This classic Italian starter salad usually comprises a selection of appetising vegetables and meats, similar to the Spanish tapas or Greek meze, and is often laid out on a large platter. My version cuts the fat but not the taste or visual appeal and can be served as either a starter or light lunch.

Serves 4 | 200 calories per portion | 13.5g fat per portion

1 tbsp olive oil

1 dsp lemon juice

2 medium courgettes, thinly sliced lengthways (see Tip)

4 canned artichoke hearts, well drained

125g ball Italian mozzarella, well drained, and torn into rough pieces

8 cherry tomatoes, halved

4 slices prosciutto (Parma ham – see Tip)

4 slices bresaola

2 fresh ripe figs, halved (optional – see Tip)

8 black stoned olives

few fresh basil leaves, to garnish

1 Mix together the oil and lemon juice, and pour this marinade over the courgettes in a bowl, stirring to combine well. If you have time, leave to marinate for 1–2 hours.

2 Preheat the grill to very hot. Place the courgettes directly on the rack, reserving the marinade, and grill for 2–3 minutes each side until softened and patterned with the rack marks. Alternatively, you can use a ridged griddle pan.

3 Fold the courgettes and arrange in two areas of a large serving platter.

4 Arrange the artichokes and mozzarella with the tomatoes, meats and figs on the platter so that they look attractive.

5 Scatter the olives over the platter and drizzle the remaining oil and lemon marinade over the tomatoes, mozzarella and artichokes. Garnish with the basil leaves and serve.

serving suggestions Crusty Italian bread makes a good accompaniment for a light lunch.

If using as a starter, a meat-free pasta dish would make a suitable main course.

tips You can use asparagus or aubergine slices instead of the courgettes, cooked in the same way.

Prosciutto is thinly sliced air-dried Italian ham. You could substitute other similar hams, such as those from Germany or four rashers of very thinly sliced, extra lean bacon, in which case the calories and fat count will be a little higher.

If you don't want to use the figs, or they are out of season, you could simply omit them (12 calories less per portion) or substitute some slices of fresh ripe mango (not authentic, but still nice!) or melon.

seafood cocktails

Old-fashioned and simple, seafood cocktails are nevertheless hard to resist. The tang of the sun-dried tomatoes gives this seafood sauce a fantastic taste and no one will be able to tell that it is low in fat.

Serves 4 | 155 calories per portion | 7.5g fat per portion

50g cos, romaine or iceberg lettuce, leaves torn

350g top quality seafood of choice, such as peeled prawns, shrimps, mussels, crab, or a mixture, clean and dried (see Tip)

1 tsp sweet paprika

4 lemon wedges, to garnish

FOR THE SAUCE

2 tbsp ready-made mayonnaise (full-fat type)

3 tbsp low-fat natural bio yogurt

1 dsp good quality sun-dried tomato paste from a jar

1 dsp lemon juice

1 dash of Tabasco

1 dash of Worcestershire sauce

1 tsp Dijon mustard

pinch of caster sugar

salt and black pepper

1 To make the sauce, mix together all the ingredients in a bowl until well combined. Taste and adjust the seasoning as necessary.

2 Divide the lettuce between four glass serving dishes.

3 Spoon the seafood on top of the leaves and pour the dressing over.

4 Sprinkle the paprika over and garnish with lemon wedges (see Tip).

tips The cocktail isn't as nice if you use poor quality seafood; try to avoid frozen bulk-buy prawns or frozen packs of mixed seafood.

Garnish with whole shell-on prawns, if you like.

creamy cheese dip with crudités

This tasty dip contains a quarter of the calories of one made with cream cheese. Yes, it contains high-fat blue cheese, but it is so tangy that a very little goes a long way.

Serves 3–4 as a starter | For 4: 70 calories per portion | 4g fat per portion
For 3: 95 calories per portion | 5.5g fat per portion

1 tbsp light mayonnaise

20ml ricotta cheese

20ml fromage frais, 0% fat

1 tbsp low-fat soft cheese

25g Dolcelatte cheese (see Tip)

20ml skimmed milk

1 tsp Dijon mustard

squeeze of lemon juice

1 dsp chopped fresh chives

salt and black pepper

FOR THE CRUDITÉS

2 sticks celery, cut into 5cm lengths

2 hearts of little gem lettuce, leaves separated

5cm piece of cucumber, deseeded and cut into sticks

4 spring onions, cut into 5cm lengths

1 medium carrot, cut into 5cm lengths

2 grissini sticks, halved

1 In a mixing bowl, beat together the first five ingredients thoroughly, then add the skimmed milk and mix again.

2 Stir in the mustard, lemon juice and chives and season to taste. If the mixture seems too thick, thin with a little extra skimmed milk to a good dipping consistency.

3 Serve the dip in ramekins with the vegetable crudités and the grissini sticks.

serving suggestion This is good as part of a party buffet and also makes a nice topping for a baked potato or a low-fat cheese sandwich filling with salad.

tip If you can't find Dolcelatte cheese, use St Agur, Roquefort or any tangy soft blue cheese, although Stilton is a bit too hard to mix well.

The dip will keep for a day or two, covered, in the fridge.

snacks and starters

ⓥ mixed pepper bruschetta

This is an ideal Italian starter to serve before roast cod, or lamb stew with lemon and tomato, for example.

Serves 4 | 190 calories per portion | 5g fat per portion

2 medium red peppers (about 100g each), halved and deseeded

2 medium yellow peppers (about 100g each), halved and deseeded

2 cloves garlic, peeled

1 tbsp olive oil

1 tsp balsamic vinegar

salt and black pepper

8 × 1cm thick slices ciabatta bread (about 200g total weight)

fresh basil and mint, to garnish

1 Preheat the grill to high and grill the peppers for 15 minutes or until slightly charred and softened. Transfer to a bowl, cover and set aside to cool.

2 When cool, peel off the skins (over the bowl, as the tasty juices will escape while you are doing this) and cut the peppers into strips lengthways.

3 Return the peppers to the bowl. Crush one of the garlic cloves and add this to the bowl with half the oil, the vinegar and seasoning. Stir very well and then tip the pepper mixture into a small non-stick pan and keep warm over a medium-low heat while you toast the bread.

4 Toast or bake the slices of bread until golden, rub with the remaining whole garlic clove and drizzle with the rest of the oil. Put the toasts on serving plates and top with the pepper mixture, including all the juices (see Tip). Garnish with fresh basil and mint, and serve immediately.

serving suggestion Basic bruschetta (bread, baked or toasted, rubbed with garlic and drizzled with oil) is very good with soup or a salad.

tip For a more substantial snack or to add protein, crumble 25g feta cheese or break up 25g Italian mozzarella or grate 15g Parmesan per person over the top of the peppers. This will add about 70 calories and 5g fat per portion.

marinated garlic mushrooms

This is a quick and easy starter for when you have friends round, but try to leave the mushrooms to marinate in the liquor for several hours.

Serves 4 | 70 calories per portion | 5.5g fat per portion

20ml olive oil

3 large cloves garlic, very finely chopped

1 tsp ground coriander seeds

250g small mushrooms or mixed wild mushrooms (see Tip)

2 tbsp lemon juice

100ml passata

1 tsp soft dark brown sugar

salt and black pepper

chopped fresh coriander, to garnish

1 Heat the oil in a non-stick frying pan and sweat the garlic over a medium heat for a few minutes; add the ground coriander and stir for a minute more. Add the mushrooms and stir to coat.

2 Add the remaining ingredients, except the fresh coriander, and bring to a simmer, then take off the heat and leave to cool.

3 Pour into a lidded, non-metallic container and refrigerate for a few hours or overnight. If the marinade doesn't completely cover the mushrooms, stir occasionally.

4 To serve, heat the contents of the container (if it is microwaveable, you can do this on medium microwave power for about 3 minutes). Divide the mushrooms between small serving dishes and garnish with chopped fresh coriander.

serving suggestions The mushrooms are also good served cold.

Crusty bread makes the best accompaniment, to mop up the garlicky sauce.

tip Try to find the tastiest mushrooms that you can – often the very small supermarket button mushrooms lack flavour. In fact, large sliced mushrooms will taste just as good here but won't look quite so pretty in the dish!

ⓥ crisp potato skins with chilli salsa

These potato skins make a nice lunch snack and are very easy to prepare.

Serves 4 | 180 calories per portion | 1g fat per portion

3 medium washed baking potatoes (about 275g each)

cooking oil spray

20g sachet fajita seasoning

FOR THE CHILLI SALSA

250g ripe tomatoes, deseeded and chopped

1 small red onion, finely chopped

1 large mild red chilli, deseeded and finely chopped

6cm piece of cucumber, deseeded and finely chopped

juice of 1 lime

salt and black pepper

1 Bake the potatoes in a preheated oven, 200°C/400°F/Gas 6, for 1 hour or until cooked all the way through (see Tip). Remove from the oven and leave until cool enough to handle. Don't turn the oven off.

2 Meanwhile, make the salsa. Put the tomatoes in a bowl with the onion, chilli, cucumber, lime juice and seasoning, stir well, cover and refrigerate.

3 When the potatoes are cool, halve them lengthways and scoop out most of the flesh with a tablespoon, leaving about 0.5cm of flesh still attached to the skin. Cut each skin half into four pieces lengthways so that you have 24 skin wedges altogether.

4 Spray the potato skins well with the cooking oil, then sprinkle the fajita seasoning over them. Place them on a good quality baking tray and bake in the preheated oven for 25 minutes or until the skins are crisp and golden. Serve immediately with the salsa.

serving suggestion Liven up plainly baked fish or chicken with these potato wedges and salsa.

tip Push a metal skewer through the potatoes to hasten cooking.

ⓥ guacamole toasts

This vitamin E-rich snack also makes a good starter, especially before a chilli con carne or tagine.

Serves 4 | 190 calories per portion and 12.5g fat per portion

2 medium tomatoes, peeled, deseeded and chopped (see Tip)

2 small avocados or 1 large, halved, stoned and peeled

1 clove garlic, crushed

1 green chilli, deseeded and very finely chopped

dash of Tabasco (see Tip)

juice of 1 lime

1 small handful fresh coriander, chopped

salt and black pepper

4 slices brown bread from a small loaf, crusts removed

10g vegetarian low-fat spread

4 sprigs of fresh coriander, to garnish

1 Add the tomatoes and avocados to the mixing bowl with the remaining ingredients, except the bread, spread and garnish.

2 Combine the mixture well with a fork until you have a rough purée of dipping consistency, with a few pieces of avocado still apparent.

3 Toast the bread, then halve diagonally and cover with the low-fat spread, then arrange on four serving plates. Top each with a quarter of the avocado mixture and garnish with a coriander sprig.

serving suggestions The guacamole makes a good sandwich filling and there's no need for butter or spread. You could also add prawns or crab and lettuce.

Use the guacamole as a dip with pitta fingers or crudités.

tips Peeling tomatoes may appear quite fiddly, but it really is quite easy – make a cross with a knife on the stalk end of the tomato, place in boiling water for 30 seconds, remove and peel.

Tabasco is a well known brand of chilli sauce but any good chilli sauce will do.

snacks and starters

soups

Home-made soup is a perfect choice for people watching their fat and calorie intake. Flavour and substance come via well-made stocks, vegetables, herbs, spices and seasonings, and there is rarely any need for more than a minimum of added fat.

Soups are so versatile that they can be served as a starter, snack, lunch, packed lunch or main course and, depending on your choice, are good for both summer and winter months. The soups in this chapter reflect this diversity and you will find one suitable for any occasion and for all tastes.

Soups are usually low in cost and easy to make and the following tips will help you produce the best results:

- Use a good quality non-stick frying pan to sauté or sweat your vegetables, if necessary, then transfer them to a heavy-based saucepan for any lengthy cooking that may be required. Alternatively, use a shallow, lidded flameproof casserole (Le Creuset make a perfect one, which will last a lifetime) with sides about 5cm high and you can do the whole job in one pan.
- Invest in a good electric blender with a large goblet, as many soups taste much better if they are all, or part, blended before reheating and serving. This saves having to add thickeners and the puréed ingredients offer a much more powerful flavour.
- Soups are only as good as the quality of their ingredients – so buy the best. I would always go for organic vegetables in my soups as they really do seem to impart a better taste.

⊘ chilled cucumber soup

Serves 4 | 90 calories per portion | 5.5g fat per portion

1 tbsp sunflower or groundnut oil (see Tip)

1 medium Spanish onion, finely chopped

1 organic cucumber (about 450g), peeled, deseeded and finely chopped

800ml vegetable stock

salt and white pepper

100ml Greek yogurt

few fresh mint leaves, to garnish

1 Heat the oil in a saucepan and sauté the onion over a medium heat for about 10 minutes, making sure it doesn't colour, until well softened.

2 Stir in the cucumber, stock and seasoning, then bring to the boil. Reduce the heat, cover and simmer for about 15 minutes.

3 Allow the soup to cool a little, then purée in an electric blender or food processor. Transfer to a lidded container, stir in the yogurt and chill until needed.

4 Serve the soup garnished with mint leaves.

tips Olive oil is too strong for this soup – you need a delicate oil such as sunflower or groundnut.

Organic cucumbers have much more flavour, and a denser texture, than non-organic ones.

soups

chickpea soup with lemon

Serves 4 | 190 calories per portion | 8.5g fat per portion

1 tbsp olive oil (see Tip)

15g butter

1 medium Spanish onion, finely chopped

125g old potatoes, chopped

900ml chicken stock (see Tip)

400g can chickpeas (250g drained weight), drained and rinsed

juice of 1 lemon

salt and black pepper

chopped fresh parsley, to garnish

1 Heat the oil and butter in a medium-sized lidded saucepan and sauté the onion for at least 10 minutes over a medium heat, until softened.

2 Add the potatoes, stock and chickpeas, stir well and bring to the boil. Reduce the heat, cover and simmer gently for 15 minutes or until the potatoes have softened.

3 Transfer the soup to an electric blender or food processor and blend until smooth.

4 Return the soup to the pan, add the lemon juice and reheat. Season to taste. Serve garnished with the parsley.

serving suggestion Serve the soup with pitta wedges.

tips The soup is very low in saturated fat but, to reduce the saturates even more, you can double the quantity of olive oil and omit the small amount of butter (which does help the velvety texture).

Use fresh chicken stock, if possible, or a good quality cube.

Vegetarians can make the soup with vegetable stock; it is still very good.

courgette, bean and pasta soup

Made with typically Italian ingredients, this soup is pretty to look at, and is a simpler version of a minestrone. It makes a hearty lunch or supper.

Serves 4 | 230 calories per portion | 6g fat per portion

1 tbsp olive oil

1 medium red onion, finely chopped

1 stick celery, chopped

1 medium carrot, fairly finely chopped

1 clove garlic, crushed

2 medium courgettes, fairly finely chopped

800ml vegetable stock

400g can chopped tomatoes

salt and black pepper

100g small dried pasta shapes of choice

400g can borlotti beans, drained and rinsed (see Tip)

25g Gruyère cheese, grated

1 tbsp chopped flat-leaf parsley, to garnish

1 Heat the oil in a large, lidded saucepan and sauté the onion, celery, carrot and garlic for about 15 minutes or until softened and just turning golden.

2 Add the courgettes, stock, tomatoes and a little seasoning, then bring to the boil. Reduce the heat and simmer for about 20 minutes.

3 Add the pasta and beans, and simmer for a further 10 minutes or until the pasta is tender, adding extra stock or water if the soup looks too thick.

4 Check for seasoning, adding more salt and black pepper to taste.

5 Stir in the Gruyère and garnish with the parsley before serving.

tip You can use cannellini beans or a can of mixed beans instead of the borlotti, or omit the beans and add an extra 50g of dried pasta.

chicken noodle soup

A tasty Japanese-style soup, filling enough for a light lunch and yet very low in fat.

Serves 4 | 150 calories per portion | 2g fat per portion

1 litre chicken stock (see Tip)

1 large skinless chicken breast (about 150g)

150g oyster or shiitake mushrooms, sliced

150g pak choi

1½ tbsp miso paste

1 tbsp mirin (rice wine) or medium sherry

100g udon noodles (see Tip)

1 tbsp soy sauce

2 spring onions, finely chopped, to garnish

1 Put the stock and chicken breast into a saucepan and bring to a simmer, then cover and cook for 15 minutes. Remove the chicken and shred into thin strips; return to the pan.

2 Add the mushrooms and pak choi and simmer again for 5 minutes.

3 Combine the miso paste with a little of the hot stock and add this to the pan (see Tip); stir well.

4 Add the mirin or sherry, noodles and soy sauce and simmer for a few minutes.

5 Serve the soup garnished with spring onions.

tips For a more authentic Japanese soup use dashi (dried fish stock) powder sachets instead of the chicken stock – use 40g dashi to 1 litre of water. You could also try a good quality fish stock instead of the chicken stock.

Udon are fat, short Japanese white wheat noodles. If you can't find them, use fine egg thread noodles or rice noodles.

For a hotter note, you could add 1 finely chopped green chilli and a 1cm knob of fresh ginger, peeled and grated, to the soup at step 3.

ⓥ middle eastern vegetable soup

This soup has both Moroccan and Turkish flavours and ingredients, and contains plenty of carbohydrate for a satisfying main meal type of soup. It is very easy to make.

Serves 4 | 160 calories per portion | 4.5g fat per portion

1 tbsp olive oil

1 medium Spanish onion, finely chopped

1 tsp harissa (see Tip), or more to taste

2 medium carrots, cut into small dice

2 medium red peppers, deseeded and cut into small squares

1 medium potato, peeled and cut into 1cm dice (see Tip)

50g bulgur wheat

800ml chicken or vegetable stock

salt and black pepper

1 tbsp chopped fresh flat-leaf parsley

juice of ½ lemon

1 Heat the oil in a large, lidded saucepan and sauté the onion over a medium heat until softened and just turning golden. Add the harissa and stir for 1 minute.

2 Add all the vegetables, bulgur wheat and stock, stir and bring to the boil. Reduce the heat, cover and simmer for about 30 minutes, adding a little extra stock or water if you think it needs it.

3 Season to taste and serve the soup with the parsley and lemon juice stirred in.

tips You can buy harissa, a classic Moroccan spicy paste, ready-made in most major supermarkets. Alternatively there is a simple recipe on page 40.

You can add 75g cooked chickpeas to the soup instead of the potato, if preferred.

soups

⊗ red lentil and coriander soup

Many soups containing pulses aren't all that appropriate for summer, but this one, containing red lentils, is quite light and would make a good spring or summer soup with some crusty bread.

Serves 4 | 250 calories per portion | 6g fat per portion

1 tbsp groundnut oil

1 large red onion, finely chopped

1 clove garlic, crushed

200g red lentils

1 litre vegetable stock

2 medium carrots, chopped

1 stick celery, chopped

1 red pepper, deseeded and chopped

1 red fresh chilli, deseeded and chopped

1 pack or pot fresh coriander, stalks removed

salt and black pepper

4 tbsp Greek yogurt, to serve (see Tip)

1 Heat the oil in a large, lidded saucepan and sauté the onion for 10–15 minutes until softened, adding the garlic for the last few minutes. Add the lentils, stock, vegetables and chilli, and bring to the boil.

2 Reduce the heat, cover and simmer for 40 minutes or until the lentils are tender. Add half of the coriander to the soup.

3 Allow the soup to cool, then blend in an electric blender or food processor.

4 Return the soup to the pan to reheat and season to taste, then stir in the remaining coriander leaves and the yogurt before serving.

tip You could use half-fat crème fraîche instead of the yogurt.

♡ watercress soup

Serves 4 | 150 calories per portion | 2g fat per portion

350g old potatoes, peeled and cut into small cubes

600ml chicken or vegetable stock

2 bunches of watercress, with large or tough stalks removed

400ml skimmed milk

2–3 shallots, finely chopped

salt and black pepper

2 tablespoons half-fat crème fraîche

1 Put the potatoes in a lidded saucepan with the stock, most of the watercress, the milk, shallots and a little seasoning. Stir well, then bring to the boil. Reduce the heat, cover and simmer for 20 minutes or until the potatoes are very soft.

2 Allow to cool a little and blend in an electric blender or food processor until smooth. Reheat and add extra seasoning to taste. Stir in the crème fraîche and garnish with the remaining watercress leaves to serve.

tip You need really fresh, dark green watercress for this, and a good quality stock; you can make your own vegetable stock easily (see page 124).

♥ pea and mint soup

Serves 4 | 140 calories per portion | 3g fat per portion

400g peas, fresh or frozen
(see Tips)

1 bunch of spring onions, chopped

1 medium old potato (about 150g),
peeled and cut into small cubes

700ml vegetable stock

1 tbsp chopped fresh mint

pinch of nutmeg

salt and black pepper

2 tbsp half-fat crème fraîche

fresh mint leaves, to garnish

1 Put the peas and spring onions in a lidded saucepan with the potato, stock, mint and nutmeg, then bring to the boil. Reduce the heat, cover and simmer for about 15 minutes or until the peas and potato have softened.

2 Allow to cool a little and blend in an electric blender or food processor.

3 Return the soup to the pan to reheat and season to taste.

4 Serve with the crème fraîche, swirled in, and topped with the mint leaves.

tips You can add the whole trimmed pea pods if you are using mangetout or sugar snap peas (include the pods in the weight) or just include a few of them.

Frozen peas are surprisingly good in this recipe.

grills Most of us are now aware that grilling is one of the healthiest ways to cook meats, poultry, fish and other foods. However, plain grilled foods can err on the side of boring unless you enliven them, which is what this chapter aims to do.

One of the simplest ways to add flavour is to marinate the meat or fish before grilling. A marinade can be as quick and simple as some citrus juice and seasoning, or balsamic vinegar; steeping the food to be grilled in an acid-based marinade for as little as 30 minutes can help add flavour and tenderness. Soy sauce or a ready-made teriyaki marinade are excellent too. You'll find several slightly more elaborate marinades in the recipes that follow, but all are easy and rely mostly on ingredients that you will have in the storecupboard.

Thick, paste-type mixtures, such as harissa or chermoula, can be used to coat meat and fish before grilling for added flavour and depth. Another quick idea is to make a crust, which will often include breadcrumbs mixed with moisteners, herbs and spices.

Plain grills are easy to jazz up with a sauce – vegetable, fruit and low-fat dairy-based sauces and salsas are the answer if you need to say no to traditional, high-fat, dairy-based ones like mayonnaise, béchamel or hollandaise. You will find more ideas for easy low-fat sauces on pages 120–4.

beefburgers with tangy mayonnaise

Beefburgers have an undeserved reputation for being unhealthy and high in fat, but in fact they are rich in minerals and vitamins and can be a fairly low-fat treat, as this recipe shows.

Serves 4 | 245 calories per person | 13.5g fat per portion

450g lean beef, minced (see Tip)

1 small onion (about 100g), very finely chopped

1 egg, beaten

1 dsp dried Herbes de Provence (see Tip)

1 dsp sun-dried tomato paste (see Tip)

salt and black pepper

cooking oil spray

FOR THE MAYONNAISE

2 tbsp good quality mayonnaise

2 tbsp Total Light Greek yogurt

1 dsp capers, rinsed well, dried and chopped

1 tsp Dijon mustard

1 tsp sun-dried tomato paste

1 In a bowl, mix together the beef, onion, egg, herbs and tomato paste and season well. Form into four round burgers, about 1–1.5cm thick.

2 Preheat the grill or a griddle pan and spray the burgers lightly with cooking oil. When the grill or pan is hot, cook the burgers for 4–6 minutes, then turn and cook the other side for about 4 minutes more (see Tip).

3 Meanwhile, mix together the mayonnaise ingredients well in a bowl and season to taste.

4 When the burgers are cooked, serve with the mayonnaise.

serving suggestion Serve the burgers with a green salad and a large burger bun (about 225 calories and 4g fat) or some thick cut oven chips, or a portion of Crisp Potato Skins (see page 22). If using burger buns, fill with sliced gherkins, tomatoes and crisp lettuce as well as some of the mayonnaise. A tomato salsa would also go well.

tips If possible, get a butcher to mince you some rump steak.

If you can't find Herbes de Provence, use ordinary mixed herbs.

Buy sun-dried tomato paste in a jar, not the sort in a tube.

The length of cooking will depend on the exact thickness of the burger and the heat of the grill. The burgers should be well cooked through – slice into one with a sharp knife to make sure there is no sign of pink in the centre before serving.

turkish lamb kebabs

The cumin gives these easy-to-make kebabs a delicious flavour. The marinade would also work with pork.

Serves 4 | 285 calories per person | 16g fat per portion

2 cloves garlic, peeled

1 tsp sea salt

1 tsp ground cumin seeds (see Tip)

½ tsp ground dried chilli

½ tsp black pepper

zest and juice of ½ lemon

1 tbsp olive oil

600g lean lamb (such as leg), cut into bite-sized cubes

1 lemon, cut into wedges

1 small onion (about 100g), quartered and separated into layers

1 Crush the garlic with the salt until it is puréed (a pestle and mortar will do this job well, otherwise use a flat, broad heavy knife and a wooden chopping board).

2 Add the purée to the cumin, chilli, pepper, lemon zest and juice, and oil in a mixing bowl and combine thoroughly, then add the lamb cubes and mix well. Leave to marinate for several hours if possible (see Tip).

3 When ready to cook, preheat the grill. Stir the lemons wedges and onion into the lamb mixture for 1 minute, then thread the lamb, lemon wedges and onion on to four large or eight small kebab sticks, dividing everything up evenly.

4 Put the kebabs on a rack under the hot grill and cook for about 15 minutes, turning halfway through cooking.

serving suggestion You could serve the kebabs with a green or tomato salad.

tips Try to buy whole spices and grind them when required (a small coffee bean mill will work well), since the aroma and flavour is much better. Don't keep ground spices for more than a few weeks as they will become stale.

An ideal time to prepare marinades is in the morning before you go to work, so that when you return the marinated ingredients are ready to cook.

sticky pork spare ribs

Serves 4 | 310 calories per person | 15g fat per portion

1.25kg pork spare ribs, trimmed and cut into 8–10cm lengths

2cm piece of fresh ginger, grated

2 large cloves garlic, crushed

4 tbsp runny honey (about 60g)

4 tbsp light soy sauce

3 tbsp dry sherry or sake

1 dsp Tabasco

green salad leaves, to garnish

1 Place the spare ribs in a shallow dish.

2 Mix together all the remaining ingredients, except the salad, and pour the mixture over the spare ribs, turning to coat them thoroughly. Leave to marinate for a few hours, if possible, though the spare ribs will still be good even if you don't.

3 Preheat the grill to medium (not too hot or the ribs will burn before they're fully cooked) and grill the ribs on the rack for about 20 minutes, basting from time to time with a little marinade.

4 Meanwhile, pour the marinade into a small saucepan and heat through, bubble well for 1–2 minutes or until you have a thick coating sauce. When the spare ribs are golden and cooked through, remove them from the grill and drizzle the cooked marinade over them.

5 Serve the ribs garnished with salad leaves.

serving suggestion Serve with some plain boiled white rice or rice noodles. Rice is about 25 calories a tablespoon and rice noodles are 225 calories and negligible fat for an average 62.5g (dry weight) serving.

persian chicken kebabs

Serves 4 | 380 calories per person | 12g fat per portion

1 tsp saffron threads

2 tbsp hot water

4 tbsp Greek yogurt (about 100g)

1 tsp ground cumin seeds

1 small onion, very finely chopped (see Tip)

2 cloves garlic, crushed

salt and black pepper

500g chicken breasts, cut into bite-sized cubes

16–20 cherry tomatoes (see Tip)

1 tbsp olive oil

TO SERVE

4 wholewheat pitta breads

100g pack mixed salad leaves

1 lime, cut into 4 wedges

1 In a bowl, mix together the saffron and hot water until the colour starts to run from the threads. Add the yogurt, cumin, onion, garlic and seasoning, mix well and add the cubes of chicken, stirring to combine thoroughly. If possible, leave to marinate for a few hours or even overnight.

2 When ready to cook, preheat the grill to medium. Thread the chicken on to four kebab sticks with the cherry tomatoes, dividing them evenly.

3 Brush the chicken and tomatoes carefully with half the oil, taking care not to brush off the marinade clinging to the meat. Grill for about 5 minutes, then turn, brush again with oil and grill for another 5 minutes or until the chicken is golden and cooked through.

4 Serve with the pitta bread, salad and lime wedges.

tips If you have a food processor, chop the onion for a few seconds until it is virtually puréed. The 'juiced' onion will improve the marinade even more.

Choose cherry tomatoes that are about the same size as the chicken pieces.

spicy chicken burgers

These succulent burgers make a great change for the family from ready-made beefburgers, and are very easy to prepare and cook.

Serves 4 | 415 calories per person | 11g fat per portion

3 skinless, boneless chicken breast fillets (400g total weight, see Tip)

1 small onion, very finely chopped

3cm piece of fresh ginger, grated

1 tbsp groundnut oil

1 tbsp soft brown sugar

1 tbsp Thai fish sauce (nam pla)

1 tbsp sherry vinegar (see Tip)

TO SERVE

4 large burger buns

crisp lettuce leaves

1 tbsp half-fat Greek yogurt

2 tbsp sweet mango chutney

1 Lay the chicken fillets flat on a chopping board and, using a sharp knife, cut them into thin 0.5cm escalopes, slicing across the top of the chicken at a slight angle (see Tip). The escalopes will be varying sizes – halve any pieces that look too big to fit into a burger bun. Arrange the chicken in a glass or china shallow bowl.

2 Mix together the next six ingredients and pour the mixture over the chicken slices to coat well. Cover and leave to marinate for several hours or even overnight.

3 When ready to cook, preheat the grill to medium. Place the chicken escalopes over the base of the grill pan (not on the rack), then cook them about 5cm from the heat for 6–8 minutes, turning once, by which time they should be turning slightly golden and cooked through.

4 Meanwhile, slice the burger buns and arrange some lettuce on each base. Beat together the yogurt and chutney. Divide the chicken between the burgers and top with the chutney mixture. Serve immediately.

serving suggestion Serve the burgers with a large green or mixed salad.

tips You may only need two chicken breasts if they are large – 400g will be ample to make four burgers.

If you don't have sherry vinegar, use white wine vinegar instead, or try balsamic vinegar but halve the quantity of sugar.

When slicing the chicken, don't cut vertically down to the board as you might for stir-fries or curries; you want thin slices along the grain.

salmon steaks with a lime and spice crust

Serves 4 | 290 calories per person | 20g fat per portion

2 cloves garlic, peeled

1 tsp sea salt

1.5cm piece of fresh ginger, grated

½ tsp Chinese five spice

½ tsp ground cumin seeds

zest and juice of 1 lime

1½ tbsp groundnut oil

30g fresh breadcrumbs

1 tbsp chopped fresh coriander

4 salmon steaks (about 125g each)

green salad, to serve

1 Crush the garlic with the salt until it is puréed (this is easiest with a pestle and mortar; otherwise use a broad, flat knife blade and a chopping board).

2 Add the spices, lime zest and juice and stir well, then mix in the oil, breadcrumbs and coriander; combine thoroughly.

3 Preheat the grill to high and put a baking tray under the grill to heat.

4 Spoon the crust mixture on to the salmon steaks and smooth it over the tops neatly.

5 Using oven gloves, remove the baking tray from the heat, add the salmon steaks (crust-side up) and return to the grill immediately. Grill for about 6 minutes or until the steaks are cooked to your liking and the crusty top is golden. Serve immediately with a green salad.

tip An even quicker crust can be made using 1½ tablespoons of good quality, ready-made fresh pesto mixed with the breadcrumbs and 1 teaspoon of Tabasco.

grilled king prawns with harissa

Serves 2 | 150 calories per person | 10g fat per portion

FOR THE HARISSA PASTE

2 tbsp olive oil

4 red jalapeño chillies, deseeded and chopped

4 cloves garlic, roughly chopped

1 tbsp ground cumin seeds

1 tbsp ground coriander seeds

1 tsp salt

Tabasco, to taste

FOR THE PRAWNS

1 tbsp butter (about 15g)

1 clove garlic, crushed

1 lemon

12 large raw king prawns (about 25g each), peeled and tails left on

1 Put all the harissa ingredients in an electric blender and blend until you have a paste.

2 Mix 1 tablespoon harissa paste with the butter and garlic and the juice from a quarter of the lemon. Warm the paste until the butter is very soft and almost melting.

3 Preheat the grill to high. Thread the prawns on to kebab sticks (see Tip), and smother them in the harissa sauce.

4 Grill the prawns for about 2 minutes, then turn and grill for another 2 minutes, basting several times, until they are pink and cooked through. Don't overcook them or they will become tough.

5 Serve the prawns with the remaining lemon cut into 4 wedges.

serving suggestion Plain basmati rice or crusty bread would go well with the prawns, along with a salad of butterhead lettuce and flat-leaf parsley.

tips The harissa paste ingredients make about 4 tablespoons of paste. Transfer the remainder into a lidded container and store in the fridge – it will keep for a week or more.

You can lay the prawns in the base of the grill pan, then grill them.

If using metal kebab sticks, get flat ones so that the prawns (or pieces of fish, chicken, or whatever you are cooking) don't roll around in circles when you turn the sticks over halfway through cooking.

seared tuna steaks with lemongrass and chilli

Serves 2 | 285 calories per person | 12.5g fat per portion

1 tbsp light soy sauce (see Tip)

1 tbsp black bean sauce (see Tip)

½ tbsp Thai fish sauce (nam pla)

1 tsp Tabasco

pinch of caster sugar

1 tbsp chopped fresh coriander

1 stalk lemongrass, outer leaves removed and centre finely chopped (see Tip)

2 tuna steaks (about 150g each)

1 dsp sesame oil

green salad, to serve

1 Mix together the first seven ingredients in a shallow, non-metallic bowl, which will fit the tuna steaks nicely.

2 Put the tuna into the bowl and spoon the marinade over the steaks; cover and set aside for 1–2 hours.

3 When you are ready to cook, brush a griddle pan with a little of the oil and heat to very hot. Meanwhile, add the marinade to a small saucepan and bring to the boil and cook until reduced a little.

4 When the griddle is hot, add the tuna steaks and cook for 2 minutes without moving them. Turn and griddle the other side for a further 2 minutes (see Tip).

5 Serve the tuna steaks with the green salad and a dessertspoonful of the heated marinade. Drizzle the rest of the oil over.

tips Light soy sauce is sometimes better in recipes than standard dark soy sauce, and this is one of those occasions in my opinion.

Black bean sauce is available in small jars in most major supermarkets.

If you find a source of fresh lemongrass, buy a few stalks and store the remainder in the freezer.

Don't overcook the tuna or it will dry out – it should still be 'blue' in the centre.

casseroles, braises and stews

This chapter contains great ideas for healthy one-pot meals. Some of the dishes take longer to cook than you may be used to, but on the other hand most of the cooking time doesn't need you to be there and the preparation is almost always extremely easy, even for novice cooks.

Casseroles and stews are ideal family fare – hungry, non-waist-watching members of the household won't even realise that these recipes are low in fat as they are high on flavour and substance, but you can always give them extra carbohydrates, such as potatoes or pasta, if needed.

I have concentrated on giving you low-fat versions of traditional, much-loved, world-wide favourites, such as chilli, goulash, curries and coq au vin – those types of dishes that we all long to eat now and then but which are usually so high in fat that we feel guilty if we do – no longer!

Casseroles are an ideal way to cook low-fat cuts of meat, and also game, which is usually low in fat, as the meat is less inclined to dry out. Lastly, one-pot meals can be bulked out with plenty of vegetables and pulses to add both flavour and fibre, and are the best winter cooking method for vegetarian meals.

When slow-cooking, it helps if you have a very good quality heavy-based flameproof casserole pan with a tight-fitting lid for more consistent results. A flameproof pan also means that you needn't transfer sautéed or sweated ingredients from a frying pan to the casserole, but can do both steps in the one pan.

beef bourguignon

The classic French red wine stew can be low in fat as long as you choose a lean cut of braising steak and add lean bacon rather than streaky.

Serves 4 | 295 calories per portion | 10.5g fat per portion

cooking oil spray

100g extra-lean back bacon, cut into strips

1 tbsp olive oil

500g lean braising steak, trimmed and cut into bite-sized cubes

16 small shallots or 12 larger ones (about 250g total weight)

1 clove garlic, crushed (see Tip)

1 tbsp plain flour

200ml red wine

100ml beef stock

bouquet garni

salt and black pepper

125g small mushrooms

1 tbsp chopped fresh parsley

1 Heat a flameproof casserole (see Tip), coat lightly with cooking oil spray and fry the bacon until golden; set aside.

2 Add half the olive oil to the pan and brown the steak over a high heat, remove and reserve.

3 Add the rest of the oil and the shallots to the pan and brown them, turning frequently.

4 Add the garlic, flour, wine, stock, bouquet garni and seasoning, stir well, bring to a simmer, cover and transfer to a preheated oven, 170°C/335°F/Gas 3½, and cook for 2 hours (see Tip).

5 Add the mushrooms and half the parsley, remove the bouquet garni and cook for a further 30 minutes, then serve garnished with the remaining parsley.

serving suggestion Serve with green vegetables and mashed potato.

tips You can buy jars of good quality, ready-minced garlic, which can be used in this recipe and many others in this book.

If you don't have a flameproof casserole, cook the bacon and brown the meat and onions in a good quality non-stick frying pan, then transfer them to a casserole dish and proceed with Step 5.

You can cook this dish on the hob, although make sure it simmers very gently – buy a heat diffuser mat from a cookstore, if your hob doesn't simmer low enough.

casseroles, braises and stews

carbonnade of beef

A simple casserole which depends for its flavour on good quality beef, plenty of onions and stout or beer.

Serves 4 | 325 calories per portion | 11.5g fat per portion

cooking oil spray

500g lean braising steak, trimmed and cut into 6 × 5cm 'mini' steaks

2 tbsp olive oil

2 large onions (about 500g total weight), sliced

2 cloves garlic, crushed (see Tip)

1 tbsp brown sugar

1 tbsp plain flour

500ml stout (see Tip)

1 beef stock cube, crumbled

1 tbsp tomato purée

1 bay leaf

salt and pepper

1 tbsp chopped fresh parsley, to garnish

1 Spray a large, shallow non-stick frying pan with a little cooking oil, heat until hot and brown the meat on all sides, then transfer it to a casserole dish.

2 Add the olive oil to the pan and sauté the onions over a medium heat for about 10 minutes, or until they begin to soften. Add the garlic and sugar to the pan, stir well, reduce the heat to medium-low and cook for another 10 minutes or until the onions start to caramelise.

3 Stir in the flour and cook for 1 minute, then add the stout, stock cube and tomato purée, stir well and bring to a simmer.

4 Transfer the onion mixture to the casserole dish and mix with the beef. Add the bay leaf and plenty of seasoning, cover and cook in a preheated oven, 170°C/335°F/Gas 3½, for 2 hours.

5 Check the seasoning, remove the bay leaf and serve garnished with the parsley.

serving suggestion Boiled potatoes, dark green cabbage and carrots are delicious with the beef.

tips Garlic is used in many casseroles as it brings out the flavours without leaving a noticeably garlicky taste.

For a less rich stew, you could use ordinary beer instead of stout.

chilli con carne

Most people love chilli – this one is medium-hot, but simply by adjusting the amount of Tabasco that is used, you can easily make it milder or extra hot.

Serves 4 | 285 calories per portion | 9.5g fat per portion

1½ tbsp groundnut oil

400g lean braising steak, trimmed and cut into 1cm cubes

1 large Spanish onion, peeled and finely chopped

1 large red pepper, deseeded and cut into 1cm squares

1 clove garlic, crushed

2 fresh red jalapeño chillies, chopped (see Tip)

1 tsp Tabasco (see Tip)

1 tsp each ground cumin and sweet paprika

400g can chopped tomatoes

1 tbsp tomato purée

400g can red kidney beans, drained and rinsed

250ml beef stock

salt and black pepper

good handful fresh coriander, to serve

1 Heat half the oil in a large, lidded non-stick frying pan and brown the meat over a high heat, stirring frequently. Remove the meat from the pan with a slotted spoon and reserve.

2 Add the rest of the oil with the onion, pepper, garlic and chillies and sauté, stirring occasionally, for 10 minutes. Add the Tabasco, cumin and paprika and stir for another minute.

3 Pour in the tomatoes, tomato purée, beans, stock and seasoning, stir well and bring to a simmer, then return the meat to the pan and combine well. Taste for 'hotness' and adjust as necessary (see Tips).

4 Cover and simmer gently for 1–1½ hours or until the sauce is a rich colour and everything is tender. Check the seasoning and stir in plenty of fresh coriander before serving.

serving suggestion Serve with rice or a baked potato, a chilli salsa, and 1 tablespoon half-fat crème fraîche per person (adds 2.2g fat per portion) or light Greek yogurt (adds 0.7g per portion).

tips Jalapeño chillies are quite mild, but will be hotter if you add the seeds to the pan with the flesh, or you could choose hotter chillies such as bird's eye.

1 teaspoon Tabasco will give a mild heat – add 2 or 3 teaspoons to make the chilli hotter.

The heat of the dish increases as it cooks, so when you taste for heat before the final cooking, remember this.

You can cook the chilli in the oven; transfer everything to a casserole dish at the end of step 3.

casseroles, braises and stews

hungarian goulash

A rich and flavoursome casserole that even young children seem to enjoy.

Serves 4 | 295 calories per portion | 14g fat per portion

1½ tbsp groundnut oil

450g lean braising steak, trimmed and cut into bite-sized cubes

1 large onion, finely chopped

2 tbsp sweet Hungarian paprika, plus extra to garnish (see Tip)

1 tbsp plain flour

1 tsp caraway seeds

400g can plum tomatoes

200ml beef stock

1 small glass red wine

salt and pepper

400g old floury potatoes, peeled and cubed

2 small or 1 large red pepper, deseeded and sliced

100ml half-fat crème fraîche

1 Heat half the oil in a large, lidded non-stick frying pan and brown the meat over a high heat. Remove the steak from the pan with a slotted spoon and reserve.

2 Add the rest of the oil and sauté the onion over a medium-high heat for about 10 minutes, stirring occasionally.

3 Add the paprika and flour, stir and cook for a minute, then add the caraway, tomatoes, stock, wine and seasoning, return the meat to the pan, stir well and bring to a simmer (see Tip).

4 Cover and simmer gently for 1½ hours. Add the potatoes to the casserole with the pepper and stir well, then cook for a further 30 minutes until everything is tender.

5 Check the seasoning, stir in the crème fraîche and serve, garnished with paprika.

serving suggestion As the dish contains potatoes, you may need only a green salad or perhaps some white cabbage, but hungry family members may like to eat the goulash with plain boiled rice or egg thread noodles or pasta shapes.

tips There are various types of paprika in the shops – make sure you get good quality Hungarian paprika, which is quite mild and sweet. If you use hot paprika, the dish will probably be inedible!

You can cook the casserole in a preheated oven, 170°C/335°F/Gas 3½, in which case transfer the mixture to the casserole at the end of step 3.

gascony lamb crumble

A simple, crunchy-topped casserole with a great depth of flavour due to the red wine and anchovies.

Serves 4 | 395 calories per portion | 16.5g fat per portion

1 tbsp olive oil

500g lean lamb fillet, cut into small cubes

1 medium onion, roughly chopped

150g celeriac, finely chopped

3 cloves garlic, crushed

200ml red wine

125ml lamb stock

400g can cannellini beans, drained and rinsed

4 anchovy fillets, rinsed well and chopped (see Tip)

1 dsp tomato purée

black pepper

60g good quality white bread, roughly crumbled or chopped into small pieces

cooking oil spray

1 Heat half the oil in a non-stick frying pan and cook the lamb pieces in two batches over a high heat until brown on all sides. Remove with a slotted spoon and transfer to a fairly shallow, family-sized earthenware-type casserole dish.

2 Heat the remaining oil and sauté the onion and celeriac over a medium heat for 10 minutes until softened. Add the garlic and stir for another minute, then transfer to the casserole dish.

3 Heat the wine and stock in the frying pan and add this with the beans, anchovies and tomato purée to the casserole and stir well, mashing some of the beans with a fork as you do so.

4 Season with pepper, cover and cook in a preheated oven, 170°C/335°F/Gas 3½, for 1½ hours. Check the seasoning – the casserole is unlikely to need extra salt as the anchovies are salty.

5 Preheat the grill to hot (see Tip). Sprinkle the bread evenly over the top of the casserole, then spray with the cooking oil, and grill until the bread is golden and crispy. Serve immediately.

serving suggestion New or mashed potatoes or French bread and green beans or a salad are ideal with this dish.

tips Anchovies add a lot to the fine flavour of this casserole but you won't detect a 'fishy' smell or flavour, so try not to leave them out.

Two tablespoons (50ml) of half-fat crème fraîche can be stirred into the casserole before topping with the bread, which would add 20 calories and 2g fat per portion.

casseroles, braises and stews

lamb rogan josh

This is a fairly hot lamb curry, ideal for the winter months.

Serves 4 | 320 calories per portion | 18g fat per portion

1½ tbsp groundnut oil

600g lean lamb fillet, cubed

2 medium onions, sliced

2 cloves garlic, crushed

1 tsp cardamom seeds (see Tip)

1 tsp ground cinnamon

1 tsp ground coriander

1 heaped tbsp sweet paprika

1 tsp hot chilli powder (see Tip)

1 tbsp tomato purée

100ml good meat stock

salt and black pepper

1 Heat half the oil in a lidded non-stick frying pan or flameproof casserole and brown the lamb over a high heat, turning once or twice until browned all over. Remove the meat with a slotted spoon and reserve.

2 Heat the rest of the oil and sauté the onions over a medium-high heat, stirring frequently, until softened and turning golden.

3 Add the garlic, cardamom, cinnamon and coriander to the pan, and stir for 1–2 minutes.

4 Add the paprika and chilli powder, and stir for another minute, adding a little stock if necessary, before returning the meat to the pan.

5 Add the tomato purée and the stock plus some seasoning, stir well and bring to the boil. Reduce the heat, cover, and simmer gently for 1 hour, or until the meat is tender and you have a rich red sauce.

serving suggestion Basmati rice and a cucumber and low-fat natural bio yogurt salad are ideal with this curry.

tips You may need to buy cardamom pods, which should be split open to remove the seeds inside.

You can add extra chilli powder to taste, or 1–2 teaspoons of Tabasco.

pork and apricot casserole

Pork marries very well with dried fruits, and this casserole is good for using storecupboard ingredients.

Serves 4 | 330 calories per portion | 8.5g fat per portion

100g ready-to-eat dried apricots, roughly chopped

50g dried apples, roughly chopped

50g ready-to-eat stoned prunes, roughly chopped

150ml dry white wine

500g pork fillet, cut into bite-sized cubes

1 tbsp plain flour

1 tbsp olive oil

1 medium onion, roughly chopped

2 whole cloves

1 tsp ground cinnamon (see Tip)

150ml chicken stock

salt and pepper

1 Soak all the fruits in the wine, adding water to cover, if necessary, for 30 minutes.

2 Dredge the pork in the flour. Heat the oil in a good quality, lidded non-stick frying pan or flameproof casserole and sauté the onion and pork over a medium-high heat, stirring frequently, until the meat is browned all over.

3 Add the spices and any remaining flour and stir well, then add the soaked dried fruits and wine, stock and seasoning; stir well to combine. Bring to the boil, adding a little extra water or stock if the mixture looks too thick.

4 Reduce the heat, cover and simmer gently for 1¼ hours or until everything is tender. Check the seasoning and remove the cloves before serving.

serving suggestion Serve with cabbage, green beans and boiled potatoes.

tip You can use a whole cinnamon stick instead of the ground variety, if preferred, but remove it before serving.

chicken cacciatore

This easy Italian casserole is colourful and full of gutsy flavours.

Serves 4 | 320 calories per portion | 15g fat per portion

1 tbsp olive oil

8 skinless, boneless chicken thighs (about 800g total weight)

1 red pepper, deseeded and chopped into 1cm squares

4 cloves garlic, crushed

1 dsp sun-dried tomato paste (see Tip)

200ml dry white wine

400g can chopped Italian tomatoes

1 tbsp chopped fresh mixed herbs (see Tip)

salt and black pepper

16 black stoned olives

12 capers, rinsed and dried

1 Heat the oil in a large, lidded non-stick frying pan or flameproof casserole and brown the chicken over a high heat for a few minutes, turning occasionally. Remove from the pan with a slotted spoon and reserve.

2 Add the pepper and sauté for a few minutes over a medium-high heat until softened and golden, then add the garlic and stir for another minute.

3 Add the tomato paste, wine, tomatoes, half the herbs, and seasoning, mix everything well and return the chicken to the pan. Bring to the boil.

4 Reduce the heat to low, cover and simmer for 40 minutes or until everything is tender and the chicken is cooked through (see Tip).

5 Stir in the remaining herbs, and the olives and capers, then serve.

serving suggestion Pasta or rice and a green salad or green beans are ideal with the casserole.

tips Buy a good quality sun-dried tomato paste in a jar, not the kind in tubes.

For the fresh mixed herbs, try thyme, rosemary and oregano, or you could use thyme, basil and parsley.

If cooking the dish in a flameproof casserole, you can oven-cook it at 180°C/350°F/Gas 4, for 50 minutes, if preferred.

coq au vin

The classic French dish is high in calories and quite time-consuming to make – this version keeps the taste without the fat and is also quick to prepare.

Serves 4 | 425 calories per portion | 17g fat per portion

1 tbsp olive oil

15g butter

100g lean smoked back bacon, cut into strips

2 medium onions, thinly sliced (see Tip)

8 skinless chicken thighs (800g total weight)

2 cloves garlic, crushed

1 tbsp seasoned flour (see Tip)

2 tbsp brandy

200g mushrooms, sliced (see Tip)

½ bottle of French red wine

150ml strong chicken stock

2 tbsp chopped fresh parsley

few sprigs of fresh thyme or 1 tsp dried thyme

1 bay leaf

salt and black pepper

1 Heat half the oil with the butter in a large, lidded non-stick frying pan or flameproof casserole and cook the bacon and onions for a few minutes over a medium-high heat until the onions have softened. Remove with a slotted spoon and reserve.

2 Add the chicken to the pan in two batches with the remaining oil and brown over a high heat on all sides, then return the onion and bacon to the pan with the garlic, flour and brandy, and stir for 1–2 minutes.

3 Add the mushrooms, wine, stock, herbs and seasoning, stir well and bring to the boil. Reduce the heat, cover and simmer gently for 45 minutes or until the chicken is cooked through.

4 Transfer the chicken and vegetables to a warm serving dish using a slotted spoon and keep warm while you increase the heat and cook the sauce for a few minutes until reduced, thickened and rich.

5 Check the seasoning and remove the bay leaf, then pour the sauce over the chicken.

serving suggestion Mashed potatoes and Savoy cabbage or steamed courgettes are good with this dish.

tips You can use 12 shallots instead of the onions, which would look more attractive for a dinner party and the flavour will be a little sweeter.

Seasoned flour is simply plain flour with the addition of salt and black pepper.

For this recipe it is best to choose small chestnut-type mushrooms, which won't discolour the sauce.

casseroles, braises and stews

winter game and mushroom casserole

Venison and rabbit make excellent low-fat casseroles without drying out or becoming tough. This one is excellent for a dinner party.

Serves 4 | 340 calories per portion | 11g fat per portion

1 tbsp olive oil

600g stewing venison, cubed (see Tip)

16 small shallots, peeled

2 green peppers, deseeded and cut into squares

2 cloves garlic, crushed

1 bay leaf

few sprigs of fresh thyme or 1 tsp dried thyme

6 juniper berries

1 tbsp plain flour

50ml brandy

200ml red wine

150ml beef stock

1 tbsp tomato purée

salt and black pepper

225g chestnut mushrooms, sliced

1 Heat half the oil in a good quality, lidded non-stick frying pan or flameproof casserole (see Tip) and cook the meat in two batches over a high heat until browned all over. Remove from the pan with a slotted spoon and reserve.

2 Add the shallots and peppers with the rest of the oil and cook for a few minutes until coloured a little, then add the garlic and stir for 1 minute.

3 Reduce the heat a little and return the meat to the pan with the bay leaf, thyme, juniper berries and flour. Stir well, then add the brandy, wine, stock and tomato purée with some seasoning and stir again. Bring to the boil, then reduce the heat, cover and simmer gently for 1 hour.

4 Add the mushrooms and cook for a further 30 minutes or until the meat and vegetables are tender. Check the seasoning and adjust to taste.

serving suggestion Potato and celeriac mash and white cabbage are perfect with the casserole.

tips You can use rabbit fillets instead of the venison or a mixture of the two meats – some butchers or supermarkets stock mixed game packs.

If you don't have a heavy-duty, lidded frying pan or a flameproof casserole, use an ordinary non-stick frying pan to brown the meat and vegetables, then transfer everything to a casserole dish and cook in a preheated oven, 170°C/335°F/Gas 3½, for the same length of time.

bouillabaisse

For people who find fish boring, this is a magnificent recipe, full of colour, aroma and flavour. It would be a good supper party dish.

Serves 4 | 370 calories per portion | 10.5g fat per portion

1½ tbsp olive oil

1 large onion (about 200g), finely chopped

1 medium leek, finely chopped

2 cloves garlic, crushed

400g can peeled plum tomatoes

1 tsp fennel seed

1 bay leaf

1 sachet of saffron threads in 1 tbsp hot water

2 strips orange zest

850ml fish stock (see Tip)

salt and black pepper

450g white mixed fish fillets, cut into large chunks (see Tip)

400g mullet, bass or bream fillet (see Tip)

225g mussels in shell, cleaned and prepared (see Tip)

225g prawns or squid or scallops (see Tip)

1 tbsp chopped fresh parsley, to garnish

1 Heat the oil in a good quality, lidded non-stick frying pan or flameproof casserole and sauté the onion and leek over a medium-high heat until softened and just turning golden. Add the garlic and stir for 1 minute.

2 Add the tomatoes, herbs, saffron, orange zest, stock and seasoning, stir well and bring to a simmer. Cook, covered, for 5 minutes.

3 Add all the fish and seafood, bring back to a simmer and cook for another 5 minutes with the lid on, or until all the mussel shells have opened (discard any that don't open).

4 Check for seasoning and remove the orange peel, then, using a slotted spoon, arrange the fish and shellfish in serving bowls, distributing the different types evenly. Pour plenty of the sauce over and serve garnished with the parsley.

serving suggestion Crusty French or Italian bread, followed by a salad are all you need with the fish stew.

tips Ask your fishmonger for all the bones and surplus bits after the fish have been filleted, then use them to make your own Fish Stock (see page 124). Otherwise, use fresh chilled fish stock from the supermarket.

For the white fish fillet, try to get the tastier, meatier varieties of fish, such as monkfish or swordfish. Haddock and even cod tend to break up too easily.

Small whole fish, such as red mullet or sea bass, make this dish special, so do try to include them.

Mussels in the shell look more attractive than the shelled mussels. However, if you do use shelled mussels, reduce the weight to 150g.

Try to use fresh prawns, squid or scallops as they will make the finished dish much tastier.

casseroles, braises and stews

sweet potato and spinach curry

Serves 4 | 205 calories per portion | 5g fat per portion

1 tbsp olive oil

1 large onion, finely chopped

1 clove garlic, crushed

1 tbsp Dry Spice Mix
(see page 123)

2 large or 4 small sweet potatoes
(600g total weight), peeled and
cut into bite-sized cubes (see Tip)

250ml vegetable stock

1 large tomato, roughly chopped

salt and black pepper

300g pack ready-washed leaf
spinach, tough stalks removed
and leaves torn

1 Heat the oil in a lidded non-stick frying pan or flameproof casserole and sauté the onion over a medium-high heat, stirring frequently, until softened and just turning golden. Add the garlic and dry spice mix and stir for 1 minute.

2 Add the potatoes, stock, tomato and seasoning, and bring to the boil. Reduce the heat, cover and simmer over a low heat, stirring occasionally, for 30 minutes or until the potatoes are tender.

3 Rinse the spinach in cold running water and, with the water still clinging to the leaves, cook in a saucepan over a medium-high heat for 1 minute, stirring, until wilted.

4 Stir the spinach into the curry and cook for a few minutes without the lid, stirring from time to time. By the time the curry is ready, it should be quite dry, as most of the stock should have evaporated.

serving suggestion This curry is delicious with a lentil dhal, rice, mango chutney and low-fat natural bio yogurt.

tip You need to use the orange-fleshed sweet potatoes, not the white-fleshed yams – scrape back a little of the skin with a fingernail to make sure you have the right sort. The taste of the orange ones is much sweeter and the texture finer.

⍩ italian bean stew

Serves 4 | 250 calories per portion | 4.5g fat per portion

1 tbsp olive oil

1 large onion, chopped

2 medium sticks celery, chopped

1 large carrot, sliced into rounds

2 cloves garlic, crushed

400g can borlotti beans, drained and rinsed (see Tip)

300ml passata

1 tsp chopped fresh rosemary

300ml vegetable stock (see Tip)

1 tsp sugar

salt and black pepper

125g pasta shapes (see Tip)

1 tbsp chopped fresh parsley, to garnish

1 Heat the oil in a lidded non-stick frying pan or flameproof casserole and sauté the onion, celery and carrot over a medium-high heat for 5 minutes until softened. Add the garlic and stir for 1 minute.

2 Add the beans, passata, rosemary, stock, sugar and seasoning, and simmer, covered, for 30 minutes.

3 Add the pasta and simmer for another 15 minutes, then check the seasoning. If the stew seems a bit dry, add a little water or vegetable stock, stir and reheat.

4 Serve garnished with the parsley.

serving suggestion This is a complete meal, but you could add some crusty bread and a green salad.

tips Use cannellini beans or butter beans instead of the borlotti beans.

Use good quality vegetable bouillon, such as Marigold, or use the Basic Vegetable Stock recipe on page 124.

For a change, use wholewheat pasta shapes and cook for an extra 5 minutes or until tender.

casseroles, braises and stews

vegetable chilli

This chilli is so hearty that nobody will notice there is no meat in it.

Serves 4 | 230 calories per portion | 4.5g fat per portion

1 tbsp groundnut oil

2 medium red onions, thinly sliced

1 red and 1 yellow pepper deseeded and chopped

2 cloves garlic, crushed

2 bird's eye chillies (see Tip)

1 tsp each ground coriander and cumin seeds

1 tsp ground chilli powder (see Tip)

1 small butternut squash, peeled, deseeded and cut into bite-sized cubes

400g new potatoes, well scrubbed and cut into bite-sized cubes

2 medium courgettes, sliced

400g can chopped tomatoes

100g black-eyed beans (cooked weight, see Tip)

1 tbsp tomato purée

200ml vegetable stock

salt and black pepper

Tabasco, to taste

handful of fresh coriander, to garnish

1 Heat the oil in a large, lidded non-stick frying pan (see Tip) and sauté the onions and peppers over a medium-high heat for 5 minutes until softened and just turning golden. Add the garlic, chillies, coriander, cumin and chilli powder, and stir for 1–2 minutes.

2 Add the remaining ingredients, except the Tabasco and coriander, stir well and bring to the boil.

3 Reduce the heat, cover and simmer gently for 45 minutes or until all the vegetables are tender. Halfway through the cooking time, test the sauce for heat and add a little Tabasco, if you like.

4 Check the seasoning and serve the chilli garnished with fresh coriander.

serving suggestion Serve with rice and drizzle the curry with low-fat natural bio yogurt or with half-fat Greek yogurt, which is slightly higher in fat and calories.

tips Bird's eye chillies are quite hot, but if you like a hot curry add more to taste. You can also add more or less chilli powder.

A 400g can of black-eyed beans will provide a surplus of 150g beans – these can be frozen or mashed with olive oil and lemon juice and used as a dip.

You will need quite a large and wide lidded frying pan (or flameproof casserole) to cook this chilli – if you don't have one big enough, use a standard frying pan and after you have sautéd the onion, peppers and spices, transfer them to a large lidded saucepan with the rest of the ingredients and continue the recipe. Alternatively, transfer them to an ovenproof casserole dish and cook in a preheated oven, 180°C/350°F/Gas 4, for 1 hour or until all the vegetables are tender.

roasts and bakes

Roasting and baking are two great ways to cook meat, poultry, game and fish with little need for extra fat. However, plain roasting of low-fat cuts can give a dry and disappointing result. The recipes in this chapter add moisture as well as flavour, colour and texture, so that the finished result is always succulent.

Much of the advice previously given for grilling is appropriate for roasting – if you have time to first marinate your meat or fish, or create a crust or paste for it, the finished dish will be much more rewarding.

Low-fat oven cooking can also mean cooking 'en papillote' – wrapping the food with flavourings in a foil or parchment parcel. When you open the parcel, the aromas are stunning!

I have also used the oven to cook what many people regard as traditional fried foods, such as fish and chips, and Southern 'fried' chicken. These dishes retain all the flavour and appearance without the fat.

Most of the recipes include tips and variations so that you need never serve up a 'boring' roast again.

moussaka

This recipe for the Greek favourite reduces the fat in the traditional recipe by two-thirds – though it is still higher than many main courses in this book! However, it's well within bounds for an average low-fat maintenance diet, so enjoy.

Serves 4 | 420 calories per portion | 23.5g fat per portion

2 medium aubergines, sliced into 1cm rounds

½ tbsp olive oil

salt and black pepper

350g lean lamb, minced

1 large onion, finely chopped

1 clove garlic, finely chopped

1 tsp dried oregano

1 tsp ground cinnamon

1 tbsp tomato purée

150ml beef stock (see Tip)

FOR THE TOPPING

400ml skimmed milk

30g sauce flour

1 tsp dry mustard

80g Gruyère cheese, grated (see Tip)

1 medium egg, beaten (see Tip)

25g fresh white breadcrumbs

1 Brush the aubergines with the oil and season. Place on a baking tray and roast in a preheated oven, 180°C/350°F/ Gas 4, for about 20 minutes until softened and just turning golden; set aside.

2 Put the lamb into a good quality non-stick frying pan and heat gently for 5 minutes, so that the fat begins to run out and the meat cooks in its own fat, stirring from time to time. Add the onion and garlic and cook over a medium heat, stirring again, for a further 10 minutes.

3 Add the oregano, cinnamon, tomato purée and stock, and bring to the boil. Reduce the heat, cover and simmer over a medium heat for 30 minutes.

4 Meanwhile, make the topping sauce. Pour the milk into a non-stick saucepan, add the flour, mustard and seasoning and whisk constantly over a medium heat until the milk begins to simmer and the sauce thickens. Add two-thirds of the grated cheese and stir until it melts. Take off the heat, check the seasoning, add the beaten egg, stir well to combine and set aside.

5 When the lamb mixture is cooked, spoon it into a family-sized pie dish, top with the aubergine slices to cover the meat completely, and pour the sauce over the top. Combine the breadcrumbs with the remaining grated cheese and sprinkle it over the top of the aubergines. Increase the heat to 190°C/375°F/Gas 5, and bake for 25 minutes or until the top is golden.

tips Swap half the stock for red wine, for few extra calories and no more fat.

If you swap the Gruyère cheese for half-fat Cheddar this will save you 30 calories and nearly 4g fat per portion, but it won't be as tasty.

Don't omit the egg – it makes the topping authentically 'wobbly firm'.

chinese oven-barbecued pork with stir-fried vegetables

Pork fillet is a great meat for fat-watchers as it is so lean – this recipe adds a little 'healthy' oil and bags of flavour.

Serves 4 | 265 calories per portion | 10g fat per portion

450g pork fillet (tenderloin), cut into 1cm slices

60ml hoisin sauce (see Tip)

30ml soy sauce

2 tbsp runny honey

2 tbsp sake or dry sherry

1 tsp Chinese five spice

1 tsp wholegrain mustard

1 tbsp groundnut oil

FOR THE STIR-FRIED VEGETABLES

½ tbsp sesame oil

8 medium spring onions, halved lengthways

1 medium carrot, cut into julienne strips

100g fresh beansprouts

1 small leek, cut into thin 5cm strips

50g mangetout or fine beans

1 Arrange the pork in a single layer in the base of a shallow, non-metallic dish.

2 Mix together the next seven ingredients in a small bowl, then pour the mixture over the pork and make sure everything is thoroughly coated. Leave, covered, in the fridge to marinate for a few hours or overnight.

3 Put the pork and some of the marinade in a small roasting pan (see Tip) and roast in a preheated oven, 180°C/350°F/Gas 4, for 25 minutes, basting once or twice.

4 Towards the end of the cooking time, heat a wok or non-stick frying pan with the sesame oil and stir-fry the vegetables for 3 minutes, adding 1 tablespoon of the pork marinade for the last minute of cooking time. Serve the pork with the vegetables.

serving suggestion Serve with plain boiled white rice or white rice noodles.

tips Hoisin sauce is widely available in jars at supermarkets.
Make sure that the roasting pan isn't too large for the amount of pork, otherwise the juices will dry out.

chicken, bacon and mushroom parcels

This easy but impressive supper is perfect if friends come round to eat – take the parcels to the table.

Serves 4 | 230 calories per portion | 9g fat per portion

juice of 1 lemon

100ml (1 small glass) dry white wine

1 tbsp finely chopped fresh flat-leaf parsley, plus extra to garnish

½ tbsp finely chopped fresh thyme (or 1 tsp dried)

salt and black pepper

200g small chestnut mushrooms, thinly sliced (see Tip)

2 cloves garlic, crushed

15g butter, softened

4 skinless, boneless chicken breasts (about 125g each)

4 rashers extra-lean back bacon (about 100g total weight), cut into thin strips

cooking oil spray (see Tip)

1 Mix together the lemon juice, wine, herbs and seasoning in a bowl, and stir well. Add the mushrooms and mix well.

2 Mash the garlic into the butter with a little seasoning.

3 Place each chicken breast in the centre of a piece of foil, which is large enough to wrap the meat loosely. Bring the foil up around the chicken to make a loose bowl shape, then divide the wine and mushroom mixture evenly between the parcels, spooning it over the top of the breasts.

4 Divide the garlic butter between the four parcels, putting a knob on top of each chicken portion, then seal securely but not too tightly, leaving an 'air gap'.

5 Bake the parcels in a preheated oven, 200°C/400°F/ Gas 6, for 25–30 minutes or until everything is cooked through. Meanwhile, fry the bacon strips in a non-stick pan, sprayed with a little cooking oil until crisp.

6 To serve, put each parcel on a plate and open slightly. Divide the bacon between the parcels, sprinkling it over the top of the chicken. Serve immediately, garnished with extra parsley.

serving suggestion Serve the chicken parcels with baked or mashed potatoes and broccoli.

tips You can use any tasty mushrooms, but avoid those with very dark open gills, as they will turn the juices in the parcels an unappetising greyish-brown colour. The small button mushrooms are quite tasteless and best avoided.

Cooking oil spray is available in supermarkets, usually positioned near the bottles of oil; it contains only 1 calorie and 0.1g fat per spray, and is enough to prevent foods sticking during cooking.

tandoori chicken

Serves 4 | 225 calories per portion | 7.5g fat per portion

juice of ½ lemon

1 medium onion, cut into chunks

3 cloves garlic, crushed

2.5cm piece of fresh ginger, chopped

1 tbsp turmeric

1 tsp paprika

2 red chillies, deseeded

1 tbsp garam masala

200ml low-fat natural bio yogurt

2 skinless, bone-in free-range chicken breasts (about 175g each), halved

4 large skinless, bone-in free-range chicken thighs (about 100g each)

1 lemon, cut into 4 wedges

1 Blend the first eight ingredients together in an electric blender, adding a little of the yogurt if the mixture is too thick to blend well.

2 Stir the rest of the yogurt in thoroughly to combine. Coat all the chicken pieces and arrange them in a roasting dish. If possible, cover and leave in a cool place to marinate for a few hours.

3 Arrange the chicken on a solid baking tray, and roast in a preheated oven, 200°C/400°F/Gas 6, uncovered, for 25–30 minutes or until the chicken is cooked through and the juices run clear (the breasts may cook more quickly than the thighs, in which case remove them and keep warm).

4 Serve the chicken with the lemon wedges.

serving suggestion Serve the chicken with a tomato, onion, cucumber and coriander salad, as well as chapatis or basmati rice.

roasts and bakes

southern-baked chicken drumsticks

Serves 4 | 405 calories per portion | 20g fat per portion

100g fresh white breadcrumbs

40g Gruyère cheese, grated (see Tip)

1 tbsp finely chopped fresh oregano, or 1 tsp dried

salt and black pepper

150g fromage frais, 8% fat

50ml half-fat (light) mayonnaise

1 clove garlic, crushed (see Tip, page 43)

1 dsp sun-dried tomato paste

1 tbsp Dijon mustard

8 skinless, bone-in chicken drumsticks (about 100g each)

1 In a shallow bowl, mix together the breadcrumbs, cheese, oregano and seasoning.

2 In another bowl, mix together the fromage frais, mayonnaise, garlic, tomato paste and mustard with a little more seasoning.

3 Pat the chicken drumsticks dry with kitchen paper, then coat each one first in the fromage frais mixture, then in the breadcrumb mixture, laying each one on a solid baking tray as you do so.

4 Bake in a preheated oven, 180°C/350°F/Gas 4, for 45 minutes or until the coating is golden and the chicken is cooked through – the juices should run clear when the chicken is pricked with a sharp knife or skewer.

5 Serve the chicken hot or cold.

serving suggestion Serve with Crisp Potato Skins (see page 22), plus a tomato salsa.

tips I like to use Gruyère cheese for cooking as it is tastier than many other hard cheeses; a little goes a long way, and it also melts well.

fish and chips

In this recipe, both the fish and the chips are baked, so they are not oily and there are no fishy cooking odours but still plenty of flavour. If you choose the baked cherry tomatoes as an accompaniment, you have a complete meal cooked in the oven.

Serves 4 | 475 calories per portion | 8.5g fat per portion

4 old potatoes (about 200g each), cut into wedges lengthways

1 tbsp groundnut or olive oil

salt and black pepper

1 tbsp olive oil

1 medium onion, finely chopped

1 clove garlic, finely chopped

150g coarse fresh breadcrumbs

1 tsp dried oregano

1 tbsp chopped fresh parsley

grated zest of 1 lemon

2 tbsp seasoned plain flour

2 egg whites, lightly beaten

4 haddock fillets (about 175g each), skin on (see Tip)

1 lemon, cut into wedges, to serve

1 Toss the potatoes in the groundnut or olive oil and season well. Place them on a solid baking tray and cook in a preheated oven, 200°C/400°F/Gas 6, for 30 minutes or until golden and crisp on the outside and cooked all the way through (see Tip).

2 Meanwhile, heat the oil in a non-stick frying pan and sauté the onion for a few minutes until softened and just turning golden. Stir in the garlic and cook for 1 minute, then stir in the breadcrumbs, herbs and lemon zest.

3 Spoon the flour on to a flat plate and place the egg whites in a shallow bowl.

4 Dip each haddock fillet first in the flour, then the egg whites and finally the breadcrumb mixture (don't coat the skin/underside). As you do so, lay each fillet on a solid baking tray, then put in the oven with the potatoes for the last 15 minutes of cooking until the crusts are golden and the fish is cooked through. Serve with the lemon wedges.

serving suggestion Serve with peas or roast cherry tomatoes. Put 400g cherry tomatoes in a baking dish, sprinkle with a little olive oil and seasoning, and roast with the potato wedges.

tips Haddock is my favourite 'frying' fish but cod fillets are fine in this recipe too.

If you have time, parboil the potato wedges for 3–4 minutes, drain well and pat dry before tossing in the olive oil – this tends to make the flesh slightly softer, while giving a crisper outer coating.

roasts and bakes

baked cod with mediterranean topping

Mediterranean flavours work well for people following low-fat or low-calorie diets, as they are so full of punch and give plenty of tastebud satisfaction – second only to Asian food in that respect.

Serves 4 | 225 calories per portion | 3.5g fat per portion

1 tbsp olive oil

1 medium onion, finely chopped

2 red peppers, deseeded and cut into small chunks

2 cloves garlic, crushed

1 red chilli, deseeded and finely chopped (see Tip)

400g can chopped tomatoes

1 tbsp tomato purée

pinch of brown sugar

salt and pepper

4 cod fillets (about 175g each)

8 black stoned olives, halved

chopped fresh parsley or basil, to garnish

1 Heat the oil in a non-stick frying pan and sauté the onion and peppers until softened and just turning golden. Add the garlic and chilli, and sauté for another minute.

2 Add the tomatoes, tomato purée, sugar and seasoning. Sauté over a low to medium heat for 30 minutes, stirring from time to time, or until the mixture is rich and has a thick sauce consistency.

3 Pat the cod fillets dry and place, skin-side down, on a baking tray. Spoon the sauce on top of each fillet and scatter the olives on top. Bake in a preheated oven, 180°C/350°F/Gas 4, for 15 minutes or until the cod is cooked through but still moist inside. Serve garnished with the parsley or basil.

serving suggestion New potatoes and green beans are ideal partners to the cod.

tip Omit the chilli, if preferred.

salmon fishcakes

We should all try to eat oily fish once or twice a week, and these fishcakes are an ideal way to get people who think they don't enjoy fish to love it. The saturated fat content is less than 4g a portion.

Serves 4 | 320 calories per portion | 16.5g fat per portion

400g old potatoes, peeled and cut into chunks (see Tip)

400g salmon fillet

2 tbsp half-fat mayonnaise

2 tbsp fromage frais, 8% fat

1 dsp basil pesto

1 green chilli, deseeded and very finely chopped

handful of fresh coriander

salt and black pepper

1 tbsp plain flour

½ tbsp olive oil

1 Cook the potatoes in boiling salted water until just tender. Meanwhile, place the salmon on a plate and microwave on medium-high for 4 minutes or poach gently in simmering water for a few minutes until just cooked (don't overcook or the cakes will be dry). Remove and discard the skin and flake the fish gently; reserve.

2 When the potatoes are cooked, drain and tip them into a large mixing bowl, then roughly mash so that you still have some small lumps left.

3 Stir the mayonnaise and fromage frais into the potato, then add the pesto, chilli, coriander and plenty of seasoning. Fold in the salmon, retaining whole flakes if you can.

4 Sprinkle the flour on to a chopping board, and make eight small cakes with the fish mixture, doing this as lightly as you can – you want a rustic look. Coat both sides of the cakes with the flour.

5 Brush both sides of the cakes with the oil, then, using a metal spatula, transfer them to a non-stick baking tray and bake in a preheated oven, 190°C/375°F/Gas 5, for 15 minutes or until lightly golden, turning carefully halfway through. Serve immediately.

serving suggestion Serve with a green salad and some Chilli Salsa (see page 22).

tip Use old, floury potatoes, such as King Edwards, to make the cakes.

roasts and bakes

[♥] potato parmigiana

Serves 4 | 250 calories per portion | 11g fat per portion

450g old potatoes, peeled and thickly sliced

1 large aubergine (about 300g), cut into 1cm thick slices

2 tbsp olive oil

salt and black pepper

1 medium onion, sliced

2 cloves garlic, crushed

400g cán chopped tomatoes

1 heaped tbsp tomato purée

good handful of fresh basil

1 ball half-fat mozzarella cheese, thinly sliced

1 tbsp grated Parmesan cheese

green salad, to serve

1 Parboil the potatoes in salted water for about 6 minutes until just tender, then drain.

2 Meanwhile, toss the aubergine in half of the oil, season and arrange the slices on a solid tray. Roast in a preheated oven, 190°C/350°F/Gas 5, for 20 minutes or until golden and just tender.

3 While the potatoes and aubergines are cooking, heat the rest of the oil in a non-stick frying pan and sauté the onion until softened and just turning golden. Add the garlic and stir for a minute, then add the tomatoes, tomato purée, basil and seasoning; stir well.

4 Arrange half the aubergine slices in the base of a family-sized ovenproof dish, followed by half the tomato sauce, then half the potatoes. Repeat the layers and top with the mozzarella and Parmesan.

5 Bake in a preheated oven, 190°C/375°F/Gas 5, for 20 minutes or until the cheese has melted. Serve immediately with the salad.

⊗ summer vegetable gratin

Serves 4 | 260 calories per portion | 17g fat per portion

2 tbsp olive oil

2 red onions, sliced

2 yellow peppers, deseeded and sliced

2 medium courgettes, cut into 0.5cm thick slices

2 cloves garlic, crushed

1 small aubergine, cut into 0.5cm thick slices

250g fresh ripe tomatoes, halved or quartered, if large

250g chestnut mushrooms, sliced

75ml passata

salt and black pepper

1 large free-range egg, beaten

250g Greek yogurt

3 tbsp grated Parmesan cheese (about 30g)

pinch of ground nutmeg

1 Heat half the oil in a large non-stick frying pan or wok and sauté the onions, peppers and courgettes over a high heat, stirring constantly, until tender and turning golden.

2 Add the garlic and aubergine with the rest of the oil and stir-fry for a few more minutes, adding a little water if the mixture becomes too dry.

3 Add the tomatoes, mushrooms, passata and seasoning and stir-fry for a few minutes more over a medium heat, again adding a little water if necessary.

4 Tip the mixture into a family-sized baking dish and smooth the top.

5 Beat together the egg, yogurt, half the cheese, nutmeg and seasoning, and pour the mixture over the vegetables (see Tip). Sprinkle the rest of the Parmesan over the top.

6 Bake in a preheated oven, 190°C/375°F/Gas 5, for 30 minutes or until golden and bubbling. Serve immediately.

serving suggestion Serve with a large green salad and new potatoes.

tip This yogurt coating also makes a simple, relatively low-fat topping for Moussaka (see page 58).

roasts and bakes

winter root vegetable bake

This dish makes an easy one-pan supper for all the family.

Serves 4 | 320 calories per portion | 16.5g fat per portion

2 red onions, quartered

2 large carrots, cut into bite-sized chunks

2 parsnips, cut into bite-sized chunks

1 butternut squash, peeled, deseeded and cut into bite-sized chunks

250g potatoes, peeled and cut into bite-sized chunks

4–6 several cloves garlic, unpeeled

1½ tbsp olive oil

salt and black pepper

1 heaped tsp mixed dried herbs

100g ricotta cheese

200g Greek yogurt

1 free-range egg, beaten

2 tbsp grated Parmesan cheese (see Tip)

400g can chopped tomatoes

1 Put all the root vegetables and the garlic into a large roasting pan and toss well with the oil. Season well and sprinkle the herbs over the top. Bake in a preheated oven, 190°C/375°F/Gas 5, for 30 minutes, or until the vegetables are almost tender when pierced with a sharp knife, turning once.

2 Meanwhile, mix together the ricotta, yogurt, egg, Parmesan and some seasoning.

3 Remove the vegetables from the oven and pour the tomatoes over the top (they won't cover everything thoroughly but that doesn't matter). Reduce the heat to 180°C/350°F/Gas 4.

4 Pour the yogurt mixture over the top – again, it won't completely cover the vegetables. Return the pan to the oven and cook for a further 20 minutes or until the topping is set and golden and all the vegetables are tender.

serving suggestion This is a meal in itself but you could serve small portions of it with some lean roast beef or chicken.

tip Use Parmigiano Reggiano Parmesan cheese, not the ready-grated kind in tubs, which tends to be tasteless.

quick hob suppers

During the week, most people need a quick meal – something that is no hassle to put together and will be on the table in a matter of minutes.

All recipes in this chapter fulfil these criteria – indeed, many take no more than 15–20 minutes from start to finish, and at most 30 minutes. All are cooked using minimal equipment, usually just one pan.

However, there the similarities end. You'll find a wide variety of tastes, flavours and ingredients in dishes made famous in all corners of the world, from Thai curries to Mediterranean dishes to Chinese stir-fries. There are ideas from Mexico, France, Spain, Africa and more.

A really good quality non-stick frying pan is the only real essential you may need to buy to make the following recipes – it will help to keep down the amount of fat you need to add to any dish and makes for more even and speedy cooking. You could also take some time to go through your storecupboard and stock up on ingredients that you'll call on time and time again for making quick, healthy meals, such as cooked pulses, cans of tomatoes, spices, herbs and seasonings.

Most of the quick hob suppers serve two but can easily be halved for lone diners and, if you have a really large pan, can be doubled to serve a family. You will find other ideas for quick suppers in the Grills (see page 33), Salads (page 101) and Pasta, Rice and Grains (page 91) chapters.

beef stroganoff

Possibly one of the most delicious quick suppers that you could rustle up. Although it is indulgent with ingredients, such as brandy and beef, it is still well within the boundaries of a low-fat main meal.

Serves 2 | 375 calories per portion | 18g fat per portion

1 tbsp olive oil

1 medium onion, finely chopped

300g lean rump steak, cut into thin strips

1 tsp Hungarian paprika (see Tip)

1 tsp sauce flour

200g small mushrooms, thinly sliced

1 tbsp brandy

50ml beef stock

salt and black pepper

100ml full-fat Greek yogurt

1 tbsp chopped fresh parsley, to garnish

1 Heat half the oil in a non-stick frying pan and sauté the onion over a medium-high heat for 10 minutes or until softened and just turning golden, then remove with a slotted spoon and reserve.

2 Add the rest of the oil to the pan, turn the heat up to full and sear the meat in two batches until browned on all sides – make sure the heat is high so that this will take only 1–2 minutes per batch.

3 Reduce the heat a little and return the first batch of meat and the onions plus all the juices to the pan, then add the paprika and flour and stir for 1–2 minutes.

4 Add the mushrooms, brandy, stock and seasoning, stir well, then bring to the boil. Reduce the heat and simmer gently on a low heat for 3 minutes, uncovered.

5 Stir in the Greek yogurt and warm through, then serve garnished with the parsley.

serving suggestion Flat noodles or a mixture of long-grain and wild rice and a green salad go well with the beef.

tip If you haven't got any Hungarian paprika, which is quite sweet, use 1 teaspoon Dijon mustard instead.

steak au poivre

There is no reason why you can't have an occasional juicy steak on a low-fat plan – lean beef is low in both total fat and saturated fat.

Serves 2 | 295 calories per portion | 11g fat per portion

100ml beef stock

cooking oil spray

2 lean sirloin steaks (about 200g each)

salt

1 tsp roughly crushed black peppercorns (see Tip)

2 tbsp brandy

2 tbsp half-fat crème fraîche

1 Put the stock in a heavy non-stick frying pan and boil vigorously over a high heat until it has reduced by half – this concentrates the flavours. Pour it into a jug and clean the pan with kitchen paper.

2 Reheat the pan and spray lightly with cooking oil. Sprinkle the steaks with salt and half the peppercorns and cook them on a high heat for 2 minutes each side (for medium rare) or to suit your preference (see Tip).

3 Transfer the steaks to warm plates, add the brandy to the pan and boil for 20 seconds on high. Add the stock, the remaining peppercorns and the crème fraîche, stir and, when the sauce begins to bubble, pour it around the steaks.

serving suggestion Serve the steaks with baked potato wedges or new potatoes, broccoli and mangetout.

tips You could use mixed peppercorns or pink peppercorns, if preferred.

For a rare steak, cook for 1½ minutes each side; for medium cook for 2½ minutes each side; and for well done cook for 3 minutes each side, but it also depends on the thickness of your steaks. A finger test may help – if the steak gives a lot when pressed with a finger, it is rare, and if it is resistant, it is well done.

quick hob suppers

seared ginger beef and mushrooms

Ginger is a bit like coriander – you either love it or hate it – but in most cases, people who start off hating it, end up loving it!

Serves 2 | 330 calories per portion | 13g fat per portion

1 tbsp groundnut oil

100g broccoli, cut into small florets

300g lean rump steak, cut into strips

3cm piece of fresh ginger, grated or 1 dsp ready-prepared ginger

2 cloves garlic, crushed

125g shiitake mushrooms, sliced (see Tip)

100g canned bamboo shoots, drained and sliced

FOR THE SAUCE

1 dsp sauce flour

1 tsp brown sugar

1 tbsp soy sauce

1 tbsp dry sherry

½ tbsp sherry vinegar (see Tip)

1 dsp black bean sauce

50ml beef stock

1 Combine the sauce ingredients thoroughly in a jug or bowl and set aside.

2 Heat the oil in a non-stick wok or large non-stick frying pan and stir-fry the broccoli over a high heat for 2 minutes.

3 Add the beef and stir-fry for 1½ minutes, then add the ginger and garlic and stir to combine.

4 Add the mushrooms and bamboo shoots and stir-fry for 1 minute, then tip in the sauce ingredients, stir well and cook for a further 2 minutes, stirring continuously. Serve immediately (see Tip).

serving suggestion Serve with egg thread noodles.

tips Use oyster mushrooms or chestnut mushrooms instead of the shiitake.

If you don't have any sherry vinegar, substitute white or red wine vinegar instead.

You can garnish the finished dish with fresh basil leaves.

thai style red curry

Don't be put off trying this great supper by the long list of ingredients – you are likely to have many of them already and they can be converted into a red curry paste in a few seconds using a blender.

Serves 2 | 320 calories per portion | 11.5g fat per portion

½ tbsp groundnut oil

1 red pepper, deseeded and thinly sliced (see Tip)

350g lean rump steak, cut into bite-sized cubes

200ml skimmed coconut milk

FOR THE RED CURRY PASTE

2 fresh red chillies, halved (see Tip)

1 tsp ground coriander seeds

1 tsp ground cumin seeds

2 cloves garlic, peeled

1 stalk (about 6cm) fresh or preserved lemongrass, chopped (see Tip)

1 tsp grated fresh ginger or galangal (see Tip)

2 shallots, halved

1 tsp chilli powder

½ tsp ground turmeric

½ tsp shrimp paste or 1 tsp Thai fish sauce (nam pla)

pinch of salt

1 Put all the red curry paste ingredients into an electric blender and blend to a paste, adding a little drop of water, if necessary.

2 Heat the oil in a non-stick frying pan and sauté the pepper over a medium-high heat for 5 minutes until it is softened, stirring frequently.

3 Increase the heat and add the steak; cook for 1 minute until browned on all sides, then add the red curry paste and stir over a high heat for another 30 seconds.

4 Add the coconut milk and bring to a simmer, then turn the heat down and cook, uncovered, for 20 minutes.

serving suggestion Serve with Thai fragrant rice and a mizuna salad.

tips Instead of the red pepper, you could use 1 large tomato, roughly chopped, in which case add it to the pan after the steak.

Use the chilli seeds unless you want a very mild paste. Jalapeño chillies are milder; bird's eye or Scotch bonnet chillies are hotter.

If you find fresh lemongrass, buy a whole bunch, since the stalks freeze well. You can also buy preserved lemongrass in jars in supermarkets. Don't buy dried lemongrass, which has an inferior flavour.

It is possible to buy grated ginger which has been preserved in small jars, or you could grate your own – a 2cm piece will yield about 1 heaped teaspoon of grated ginger. Galangal is the traditional Thai spice in this recipe, but is not widely available as a fresh root and the dried galangal available in small jars is not so good.

steak with garlic and red wine

Serves 2 | 325 calories per portion | 12.5g fat per portion

10g butter

1 large or 2 small shallots (50g total weight), very finely chopped

4 cloves garlic, finely chopped

2 lean sirloin steaks (about 200g each)

salt and black pepper

dash of Worcestershire sauce

50ml red wine

1 tsp Dijon mustard

1 tbsp chopped fresh parsley

1 Heat the butter in a heavy non-stick frying pan and sauté the shallots over a medium-high heat for 3–4 minutes or until softened. Add the garlic and cook for a further 1 minute.

2 Push the shallot and garlic to the sides of the pan, increase the heat to high and add the steaks, sprinkled with some salt and black pepper and a dash of Worcestershire sauce. Cook them for 2 minutes each side for medium rare, or to taste.

3 Transfer the steaks to warm serving plates, leaving behind most of the onion, and add the red wine to the pan with another dash of Worcestershire sauce, the mustard, parsley and a little more seasoning.

4 Stir well, bring to the boil and cook for 30 seconds. Serve the steaks with the sauce drizzled around them.

serving suggestion New potatoes and green beans are ideal with the steaks.

minted lamb meatballs with pitta

Serves 2 | 440 calories per portion | 17g fat per portion

200g lean lamb, minced

100g spring onion, finely chopped

1 tbsp chopped fresh mint

1 dsp tomato purée

½ tsp ground cumin seeds

salt and black pepper

½ tbsp olive oil

200g cherry tomatoes, quartered

1 tbsp light Greek yogurt

1 tbsp ready-made hummus

juice of ¼–½ lemon

2 pitta breads, to serve (see Tip)

5cm piece of cucumber, roughly chopped, to garnish

1 Mix the lamb with the spring onion, mint, tomato purée, cumin and seasoning and form into 8 small, slightly flattened balls using your hands.

2 Heat the oil in a non-stick frying pan and cook the lamb balls over a medium heat for about 10 minutes, turning once. About two-thirds of the way through the cooking time, add half of the cherry tomatoes and cook until softened, pressing them down a little into the base of the pan.

3 Meanwhile, mix together the Greek yogurt, hummus and lemon juice to taste. Season with salt and pepper.

4 Serve the lamb balls and cooked tomatoes in the pitta breads, filled with the remaining cherry tomatoes and cucumber. Drizzle the hummus dressing over and serve with extra salad.

serving suggestion This is a complete supper but you could add extra salad.

tip Wholewheat pitta breads are slightly lower in calories and higher in fibre than white pittas.

quick hob suppers

pork with pak choi and plum sauce

This is very low in calories and fat, but, served with a carbohydrate, such as noodles, makes a substantial meal.

Serves 2 | 255 calories per portion | 8g fat per portion

½ tbsp groundnut oil

225g pork tenderloin, cut into strips

1 tsp grated fresh ginger

1 clove garlic, crushed

4 spring onions, cut diagonally

1 courgette, thinly sliced

150g pak choi, roughly chopped

100g canned water chestnuts, well drained and halved (see Tip)

3–4 tbsp chicken or vegetable stock

1 tbsp soy sauce

2 tbsp plum sauce

1 Heat the oil in a non-stick wok or large non-stick frying pan and stir-fry the next five ingredients over a high heat for 4 minutes.

2 Add the pak choi and water chestnuts – and 1–2 tablespoons of stock if the mixture looks very dry – and stir-fry for another 2 minutes.

3 Add the soy sauce, plum sauce and 1–2 tablespoons of stock, stir well and heat through before serving.

serving suggestion Rice noodles or long-grain rice are simple accompaniments to the pork.

tip If you don't like water chestnuts, or can't find any, use sliced bamboo shoots or mushrooms instead.

creamy pork with peppers

A warming supper for a winter's evening.

Serves 2 | 320 calories per portion | 12.5g fat per portion

½ tbsp groundnut oil

250g pork fillet (leg or tenderloin), cut into strips

1 large red pepper, deseeded and thinly sliced

1 large or 2 small shallots, finely chopped

1 clove garlic, crushed

1 tsp sweet paprika, plus extra for sprinkling

1 tsp sauce flour or cornflour

25ml chicken stock

100g small mushrooms, sliced

100ml dry white wine

salt and black pepper

75ml Greek yogurt

1 Heat half the oil in a non-stick frying pan and cook the meat over a high heat until browned on all sides; remove and reserve.

2 Add the pepper and shallots to the pan with the rest of the oil, reduce the heat a little and stir-fry for 4–5 minutes or until softened and just turning golden. Add the garlic and paprika for the last minute of cooking, plus a little water if necessary (see Tip).

3 Add the flour and a dash of the stock and stir for about 20 seconds, then add the mushrooms, wine, the rest of the stock and seasoning, and stir well.

4 Return the meat to the pan and bring to a simmer. Cook gently for 5 minutes, then stir in the yogurt to warm through without boiling. Sprinkle with extra paprika to serve.

serving suggestion Serve with basmati rice or flat noodles and a green salad.

tip When adding water to a stir-fry as a lubricant, add only just enough to moisten the mixture – usually a dessertspoon is sufficient.

quick hob suppers

bacon, broad bean and potato supper

All age groups seem to like this starchy supper, which is particularly quick to make if you happen to have any leftover cooked new potatoes in the fridge.

Serves 2 | 415 calories per portion | 14g fat per portion

500g new potatoes, halved if large

200g broad beans from a good quality freezer pack (see Tip)

100g (4 thin rashers) lean back bacon, cut into strips

cooking oil spray

1½ tbsp olive oil

1 red onion (about 100g), very thinly sliced

1 tbsp chopped fresh mint

juice of ½ lemon

salt and black pepper

1 Parboil the potatoes in lightly salted water until just about tender; drain and reserve.

2 Meanwhile, blanch the beans in boiling water for 2 minutes; drain and reserve.

3 Cook the bacon strips in a non-stick frying pan, sprayed with cooking oil (see Tip) until golden and slightly crisp, then remove them with a slotted spatula and reserve.

4 Heat the olive oil in the frying pan and sauté the potatoes and onion over a medium-high heat, turning from time to time, until the potatoes are golden.

5 Add the beans, mint, lemon juice and seasoning to the pan, stir, reduce the heat a little and cook for another 1–2 minutes. Stir the bacon into the mixture and serve.

serving suggestion This is a meal in itself but you could add a mixed salad.

tips You could use fresh broad beans but they will need cooking a little longer unless they are very small.

When cooking the bacon, put it in a cold pan and let it heat up to allow the bacon to cook gradually in its own fat. Don't move the bacon until it has sealed on the underside or it may stick to the pan.

chicken fajitas with avocado

Serves 2 | 495 calories per portion | 19.5g fat per portion

300g skinless chicken breast, cut into strips

1 dsp Mexican fajita seasoning (see Tip)

1 tbsp olive oil

1 red onion (about 100g), chopped

1 red pepper, deseeded and chopped

1 yellow pepper, deseeded and chopped

2 tbsp Chilli Salsa (see page 22)

2 ready-made Mexican flour tortillas, to serve

FOR THE SAUCE

½ small ripe avocado, peeled, stoned and flesh chopped

2 tbsp fromage frais, 0% fat

juice of 1 small lime

salt and black pepper

1 Sprinkle the chicken breast strips with the seasoning.

2 Mix together all the sauce ingredients.

3 Heat half the oil in a non-stick frying pan and stir-fry the onion and peppers over a medium-high heat for 5 minutes until softened and turning golden. Remove from the pan with a slotted spoon and reserve in a bowl.

4 Add the rest of the oil and the chicken to the pan and stir-fry for 3–4 minutes until the chicken is cooked through, then return the peppers and onion and any juice in the bottom of the bowl to the pan to heat through.

5 Divide the chicken mixture, salsa and avocado sauce between the tortillas, then roll up and serve in napkins.

serving suggestion These tortillas are a meal in themselves.

tips Omit the chilli from the salsa if you prefer a milder taste.
Fajita seasoning can be found in small packs in the Mexican food section of your supermarket.

chicken korma

Traditional korma contains a lot of cream and butter but this version keeps the calorie and fat content within bounds.

Serves 2 | 375 calories per portion | 18g fat per portion

½ tbsp groundnut oil

1 medium onion, finely chopped

2 cloves garlic, crushed

1 tsp grated fresh ginger

¼ tsp ground cloves

½ tsp each ground cardamom, cinnamon and chilli

salt and black pepper

½ tsp saffron threads in 1 tbsp hot chicken stock

4 skinless, boneless chicken thighs (400g total weight), each cut into 4

75ml chicken stock

15g shelled cashew nuts (see Tip)

150ml full-fat natural bio yogurt (see Tip)

1 Heat the oil in a non-stick frying pan and sauté the onion over a medium heat for 5 minutes, stirring frequently, until it begins to turn golden. Add the garlic, ginger, dry spices and seasoning and stir for 30 seconds, adding a dash of chicken stock towards the end if necessary.

2 Add the saffron and soaking liquid and the chicken pieces, and stir for 1–2 minutes until the chicken is coloured.

3 Add the chicken stock and bring to the boil. Reduce the heat and simmer, uncovered, for 15 minutes until the chicken is cooked through, by which time much of the liquid will have evaporated.

4 Add the nuts and yogurt and heat through for a few seconds – do not boil.

serving suggestions Basmati rice, mango chutney and a herb salad are perfect curry partners.

A garnish of fresh coriander makes the dish look pretty.

tip For an even creamier taste, you can use full-fat Greek yogurt instead of the natural bio yogurt – if you omit the cashew nuts the calorie and fat count will be almost the same.

green chicken curry

Thai curries have virtually overtaken Indian curries in popularity for home cooking, and although they are a little more trouble, the result is definitely moreish.

Serves 4 | 265 calories per portion | 11.5g fat per portion

½ tbsp groundnut oil

8 skinless, boneless chicken thighs (800g total weight), each cut into 4 pieces

400ml can skimmed coconut milk

200ml chicken stock

handful of fresh coriander, to garnish

FOR THE GREEN CURRY PASTE (see Tip)

2 shallots or 1 small onion, roughly chopped

2–3 cloves garlic, peeled

2 stalks lemongrass, trimmed and chopped (or use preserved lemongrass in a jar)

4 green chillies, deseeded (see Tip)

2cm piece of fresh ginger, chopped (or use ready-grated ginger in a jar)

1 pack fresh coriander leaves and stalks

juice of 1–2 limes

1 tbsp Thai fish sauce (nam pla)

black pepper

1 Whiz together all the paste ingredients in an electric blender until you have a purée.

2 Heat the oil in a large non-stick frying pan or similar, and stir-fry the paste over a medium-high heat for 1 minute, then add the chicken, coconut milk and stock, then stir.

3 Bring to the boil, then reduce the heat and simmer, uncovered, for 15–20 minutes or until the chicken is tender.

4 Serve garnished with the coriander.

serving suggestion Serve with Thai fragrant rice.

tips It is hardly worth making just two portions of the green curry paste, so if you only want to serve two people, keep the surplus paste in a lidded container in the fridge for a few days, or freeze it.

Only deseed the chillies if you like a milder green curry.

quick hob suppers

chicken and basil sizzle

Basil and coriander are two of the strongest flavoured herbs but they do go well together in this quick Thai-style sizzle.

Serves 2 | 255 calories per portion | 11g fat per portion

2 cloves garlic, peeled

good handful of fresh coriander (see Tip)

good handful of fresh basil

salt and black pepper

1 tbsp groundnut oil

2 skinless, boneless chicken breasts (300g total weight), cut into strips

80g baby sweetcorn cobs, halved

2 red chillies, deseeded and finely sliced

little chicken stock

juice of 1 lime

1 tbsp Thai fish sauce (nam pla)

1 Using a pestle and mortar, pound together the garlic, three-quarters of the fresh herbs and seasoning until you have a coarse paste (see Tip).

2 Heat the oil in a non-stick wok or frying pan and stir-fry the chicken and sweetcorn for 2–3 minutes.

3 Add the chillies and the herb paste and stir-fry for 1 minute, adding a little chicken stock, if necessary, to prevent sticking.

4 Add the lime juice, fish sauce and a little more chicken stock (but you don't want a wet sauce) and stir-fry for 30 seconds until everything is sizzling. Serve garnished with the remaining basil and coriander.

serving suggestion Serve simply with rice or noodles.

tips Don't discard all the coriander stalks for this recipe, since they give a strong coriander flavour and will cook down well as long as you chop them before adding to the recipe.

If you don't have a pestle and mortar, crush the garlic on a chopping board using the flat of a heavy knife, then gradually work in the salt. Finely chop the herbs and mix everything together in a small bowl.

honeyed duck

Serves 2 | 270 calories per portion | 10g fat per portion

2 skinless Barbary duck breasts
(250g total weight), cut into slices
(see Tip)

2 tbsp light soy sauce

1 tbsp runny honey

½ tbsp sesame oil

1 red pepper, deseeded
and chopped

1 yellow pepper, deseeded and
chopped

80g sugar snap peas

6 spring onions, sliced

1 red chilli, deseeded
and chopped

1 If you have time, or can plan ahead, marinate the duck slices in the soy sauce and honey while you are at work, or for at least 1 hour.

2 Heat the oil in a non-stick frying pan or wok, and stir-fry the peppers, peas and spring onions for 3 minutes. Add the chilli and cook for another 30 seconds, adding a little water, if necessary, to stop sticking.

3 Add the duck and marinade to the pan and cook, stirring, for 3–4 minutes or until the duck is just cooked.

serving suggestion Egg thread noodles are all you need with this dish.

tip If you can't find Barbary duck, which has a much better ratio of lean meat to fat than standard duck (Norfolk-type), try to get Gressingham duck, another good meaty variety. This recipe also works well with pork fillet.

quick hob suppers

turkey and prawn stir-fry

Serves 2 | 355 calories per portion | 12.5g fat per portion

½ tbsp groundnut oil

300g stir-fry turkey meat

6 spring onions, cut diagonally

80g broccoli, cut into small florets

1 tsp grated fresh ginger

1 tsp Chinese five spice

½ tbsp sesame oil

100g oyster mushrooms, roughly torn if large

2 tbsp yellow bean sauce

1 tbsp soy sauce

juice of ½ orange

100g peeled cooked prawns

80g fresh beansprouts

dash of chicken or vegetable stock (optional)

1 Heat the oil in a non-stick wok or frying pan, and stir-fry the turkey, spring onions and broccoli over a high heat for 3 minutes.

2 Add the ginger and five spice and stir-fry for a few seconds.

3 Add the sesame oil and stir in the mushrooms for 30 seconds.

4 Stir in the yellow bean sauce, soy sauce, orange juice and prawns, and cook for another 1 minute.

5 Add the beansprouts and stir-fry for 1 minute, adding a dash of stock if necessary. Serve immediately.

serving suggestions Serve simply with egg thread noodles.

Instead of the noodles, you could mix the turkey and prawn stir-fry into Thai fragrant rice or basmati rice. The recipe will then be similar to the Indonesian dish, nasi goreng.

scampi provençal

Serves 2 | 295 calories per portion | 5.5g fat per portion

½ tbsp olive oil

2 medium shallots, finely chopped

3 cloves garlic, crushed

1 jalapeño chilli, deseeded and finely chopped

400g can chopped tomatoes

50ml (about ½ glass) dry white wine

1 bay leaf

black pepper (see Tip)

1 tbsp chopped fresh parsley, plus extra to garnish

400g peeled prawns (see Tip)

1 Heat the oil in a non-stick frying pan and sauté the shallots over a medium heat for a few minutes until softened. Add the garlic and chilli and stir for 1 minute.

2 Add the tomatoes, wine, bay leaf and pepper, stir well and bring to the boil. Reduce the heat and simmer for about 20 minutes or until you have a good sauce.

3 Add the parsley and prawns and simmer for 2–3 minutes to warm through, then serve garnished with a little extra parsley.

serving suggestion Rice and a green salad make simple accompaniments to the prawns.

tips You can use fresh raw prawns: add them to the sauce a little earlier so that they simmer for around 5 minutes and turn pink. The dish will look attractive if the tails are left on the prawns. If using cooked prawns, try to get good quality large ones.

quick hob suppers

quick crabcakes

These hot and spicy little crabcakes are easy to make. Crab is an underused seafood and very low in fat.

Serves 2 | 295 calories per portion | 14.5g fat per portion

200g crab meat

2 spring onions, finely chopped

2 bird's eye chillies, deseeded and finely chopped

3 lime leaves or 1 short stalk lemongrass, finely chopped (see Tip)

1 tsp Thai fish sauce (nam pla)

1 tbsp half-fat mayonnaise

1 handful fresh coriander

dash of Tabasco

30–40g white breadcrumbs

1 tbsp groundnut oil

10g plain white flour

1 lime, cut into wedges, to serve

1 In a bowl, mix together the first eight ingredients thoroughly, then add enough of the breadcrumbs to hold the mixture together so that you can form four small patties.

2 Heat half the oil in a non-stick frying pan. Dredge the patties with flour and fry the cakes on one side for 3 minutes.

3 Add the rest of the oil, turn the cakes over and fry for another 2–3 minutes. Serve with the lime wedges.

serving suggestion Serve with a combination of long-grain and wild rice, a tomato salad or salsa, and Thai dressing used as a dipping sauce (see page 122).

tip Lime leaves are becoming more widely available, but if you don't have them or the lemongrass, use the zest of 1 lime.

⊗ minted new potato and courgette frittata

*An omelette is often a high-fat supper, but this Italian version cuts the
fat considerably by including low-fat potatoes and courgettes,
reducing the number of eggs needed.*

Serves 3–4 | For 3: 325 calories per portion | 16g fat per portion
For 4: 245 calories per portion | 12g fat per portion

400g new potatoes, cut into bite-sized cubes

2 small to medium courgettes (150g total weight), cut into thin slices

50g baby broad beans (see Tip)

6 medium eggs

salt and black pepper

1 tbsp chopped fresh mint

4 spring onions, chopped

10g butter (about ½ tbsp)

½ tbsp grated Parmesan cheese

1 Cook the potatoes in a saucepan of salted boiling water
for 10 minutes or until tender; drain and set aside.
Meanwhile, steam the courgettes and broad beans until
just tender (see Tip); set aside.

2 Beat the eggs in a large mixing bowl with 1 tablespoon of
cold water and season. Add the mint, potatoes,
courgettes, broad beans and spring onions, and stir well.

3 Heat the butter over a medium heat in a large non-stick
frying pan, swirling it around as it melts so that it doesn't
burn. When melted, pour the omelette mixture into the
pan and use a fork to spread the vegetables evenly over
the base of the pan.

4 Turn the heat down and cook the omelette for several
minutes until the base is set and golden (use a spatula to
lift a section to see) and the top is beginning to solidify.

5 Preheat the grill to medium. Sprinkle the top of the
omelette with Parmesan and brown under the grill for
1 minute, then serve cut into wedges.

serving suggestion Serve simply with a salad.

tips Save using another pan with a collapsible stainless steel
steamer, widely available in cookshops. This fits almost any
size of saucepan, so you can steam the courgettes and beans
over the top of the potatoes as they boil.

You can vary the vegetables used – though I would say the
potatoes are essential. Try peas instead of the broad beans and
asparagus instead of the courgettes.

quick hob suppers

☺ cheese and potato rosti

If you have a food processor, you can grate the vegetables for the rosti in a few seconds.

Serves 2–3 | For 2: 455 calories per portion | 18g fat per portion
For 3: 305 calories per portion | 12g fat per portion

350g firm-fleshed potatoes (see Tip), peeled and grated

200g orange-fleshed sweet potatoes, peeled and grated

1 Spanish onion, cut into very thin semi-circles and halved again

1 clove garlic, finely chopped

½ tsp ground cumin

1 tbsp chopped fresh parsley

salt and black pepper

1 medium egg, lightly beaten

100g half-fat mozzarella cheese, grated

1½ tbsp olive oil

1 Put both types of potato in a clean teacloth and press well to remove any surplus liquid.

2 Tip the potatoes into a large mixing bowl with the onion, garlic, cumin, parsley and seasoning, and mix well.

3 Add the egg and mozzarella and mix again, then divide the mixture into 2 or 3 (depending on number to serve), or you can cook the rosti whole and cut it up when cooked (see Tip).

4 Heat half the oil in a large non-stick frying pan and add the rosti/s, pressing the mixture down well with a spatula.

5 Cook over a medium heat for 10 minutes or until the base is set and golden (lift an edge with a spatula to check). Add the rest of the oil, turn the rosti/s over and cook for a further 8 minutes or until tender all the way through and golden on both sides.

serving suggestion Serve with a simple salad.

tips You need to use waxy potatoes, not floury ones, otherwise they won't grate well.

Since the rosti mixture is very loose, don't worry if you can't form it into perfect cakes or patties; this doesn't matter, just divide it as best you can if you are serving individual rostis.

quick vegetable curry

This curry has a satisfying chunky texture and rounded flavour, so even carnivores won't miss the meat.

Serves 2 | 250 calories per portion | 8.5g fat per portion

100g frozen green beans

150g frozen cauliflower florets

1 tbsp groundnut oil

1 tbsp Dry Spice Mix (see page 123)

6 spring onions, finely chopped

2 large fresh ripe tomatoes, roughly chopped, with their juice

250g butternut squash, peeled and cut into bite-sized cubes

about 100ml skimmed coconut milk

salt and black pepper

100g fresh baby leaf spinach (see Tip)

1 Defrost the beans and cauliflower in the microwave and pat dry with kitchen paper (see Tip).

2 Heat the oil in a lidded, non-stick frying pan. Add the spice mix and spring onions and cook over a medium-high heat for 1 minute, stirring continuously.

3 Add the rest of the ingredients, except the spinach, (including enough coconut milk to come about three-quarters of the way up the vegetables), and stir well. Bring to the boil, then reduce the heat and simmer, covered, for 15–20 minutes until everything is tender.

4 Add the spinach and simmer for another 2 minutes, uncovered, until wilted, before serving.

serving suggestion Chapati, pitta or basmati rice, low-fat natural bio yogurt and tomato chutney are perfect accompaniments.

tips You can use finely shredded spring greens instead of the spinach.

Using frozen beans and cauliflower saves some time, but if you don't defrost them first, they may make the curry too watery. If you haven't got a microwave, put them in a sieve under running water and dry in a clean tea towel. You can use fresh green beans and cauliflower, but cut the cauliflower small, otherwise it may not cook through in the suggested time.

quick hob suppers

ⓥ stir-fry ratatouille with mozzarella

Real ratatouille is a stew, cooked long and slow, but this version borrows the Chinese technique to get all that flavour on your plate in less than 30 minutes.

Serves 2 | 230 calories per portion | 12.5g fat per portion

1 tbsp groundnut oil

1 medium red onion, thinly sliced

1 large yellow pepper, deseeded and thinly sliced

2 medium courgettes, thinly sliced lengthways

2 cloves garlic, finely chopped

2 large fresh ripe tomatoes, roughly chopped

salt and black pepper

about 100ml vegetable stock

100g half-fat mozzarella cheese, grated (see Tips)

few fresh basil leaves, to serve

1 Heat half the oil in a wok or large non-stick frying pan and stir-fry the onion and pepper over a high heat for 3 minutes.

2 Add the rest of the oil to the pan with the courgettes and stir-fry for another 3 minutes, then add the garlic and stir for a few more seconds.

3 Tip in the tomatoes, plus all their juice, season well, add half the stock and bring to the boil. Reduce the heat and simmer for 10–15 minutes or until all the vegetables are tender, adding a little more stock if the ratatouille looks dry.

4 Stir in the mozzarella until melted, check the seasoning and stir in the basil to serve.

serving suggestion Crusty French bread is perfect for mopping up the juices.

tips You can use ricotta cheese, which will have a slightly lower calorie count but similar fat content per portion.

Non-vegetarians could, for a change, omit the cheese and stir in 150g chicken fillet, cubed, at the start of the simmering stage. This will have a similar calorie count but nearly 3g of fat less per portion.

pasta, rice and grains

Pasta and the quick-cook grains, such as couscous, bulgur wheat and instant polenta, form a huge part of any health-conscious cook's repertoire because they are naturally low in fat, cook in minutes, are endlessly adaptable and versatile, marrying well with so many flavours and, of course, are delicious comfort food.

The only problem a fat-watcher may encounter is that pasta, rice and other grains are sometimes served with high-fat, high-calorie sauces or ingredients. Think of cream-laden pasta carbonara, cheese- and meat-heavy lasagne or butter-rich risotto, and you see what I mean!

The recipes in this chapter include most of our long-standing favourites, all 'reworked' to reduce their fat levels to an acceptable minimum; the flavour and texture remain, while the fat and calories are much lower.

There are also plenty of naturally light recipes, such as Salmon with Pappardelle and Saffron and Pasta Primavera. If you're too busy to try even a simple recipe, don't forget that you can create a quick pasta meal using a ready-made tomato sauce, or just a drizzle of olive oil and lemon juice with chopped fresh parsley and basil. You will also find some ideas for using grains in Salads, see page 101.

For successful pasta, you need a large pan and, if serving friends, a large decorative pasta bowl is a good investment. Please note that the cooking times for pasta and grains are only guidelines; since different brands vary, it is best to read the pack instructions first.

pasta carbonara

Many people think of carbonara as one of the richest, most indulgent and high-fat dishes you could choose, but this version brings it well within the parameters of sin-free eating.

Serves 2 | 490 calories per portion | 17g fat per portion

150g dried tagliatelle (see Tip)

10g butter

2 tsp olive oil

2 medium shallots, very finely chopped

3 rashers extra-lean back bacon, cut into thin strips (see Tip)

50ml dry white wine

1 heaped tbsp chopped fresh parsley

50g button mushrooms, thinly sliced

salt and black pepper

1 large egg

2 tbsp half-fat crème fraîche

1 Bring a saucepan of salted water to the boil, add the tagliatelle and cook for 8–10 minutes or according to the pack instructions.

2 Meanwhile, heat the butter and oil in a non-stick frying pan and sauté the shallots over a medium-high heat for 5 minutes, stirring. Push them to the edges of the pan, add the bacon and cook until tinged golden and crispy.

3 Add the wine, two-thirds of the parsley and the mushrooms to the pan with some seasoning. When the wine has started to boil, reduce the heat and simmer for 3 minutes.

4 While the mixture is simmering, beat the egg in a bowl, add the crème fraîche and some seasoning and combine well. By this time the tagliatelle should be cooked, so test, drain and return the pasta to the cooking pan (see Tip).

5 Add the bacon sauce with the egg and crème fraîche mixture to the pasta in the saucepan and heat gently, stirring for a minute until the egg has thickened. Serve in pasta bowls, garnished with the remaining parsley.

serving suggestion Green salad is just the thing to accompany this pasta dish.

tips When cooking pasta, especially when you have other things on the go at the same time, it's a good idea to set a kitchen timer so that you don't forget to tend to it at the end of the cooking time. Pasta quickly overcooks and the amount of time between a perfect 'al dente' and mush may be just a couple of minutes.

Vegetarians can omit the bacon and add an extra 100g mushrooms. The dish would then be about 45 calories less and 4g of fat less per portion.

lamb and pinenut pilaf

This is an easy to make, mildly spiced Turkish-style pilaf.

Serves 4 | 530 calories per portion | 19.5g fat per portion

1½ tbsp olive oil

400g lean lamb fillet (leg or neck), trimmed and cut into small cubes

2 red onions, finely chopped

1 yellow pepper, deseeded and finely chopped

225g long-grain rice

½ tsp each of ground cumin, coriander and cinnamon

salt and black pepper

25g sultanas

25g ready-to-eat dried apricots, chopped

½ tbsp each chopped fresh parsley and mint

550ml lamb stock

100ml low-fat natural bio yogurt

good handful of fresh coriander

20g pinenuts, toasted, to serve (see Tip)

1 Heat half the oil in a large, lidded non-stick frying pan and sauté the lamb over a high heat, turning once or twice, until browned. Remove with a slotted spoon and reserve.

2 Add the rest of the oil to the pan with the onions and pepper and sauté over a medium heat for 8 minutes or until softened and turning golden.

3 Add the rice, spices and seasoning, and stir for 1 minute, then return the lamb to the pan.

4 Stir in the dried fruits, parsley and mint, then the stock, and bring to the boil. Reduce the heat, cover and simmer for 30 minutes or until the lamb and rice are tender and the liquid has been absorbed.

5 Stir in the yogurt and coriander and sprinkle the pinenuts on top to serve.

serving suggestion This is a complete meal but you could serve it with some aubergine pickle.

tip Toast the pinenuts in a small, dry non-stick frying pan over a hot heat. Watch them carefully to prevent them burning and turn them over once the undersides have browned.

pasta, rice and grains

salmon with pappardelle and saffron

A delicate yet rich-tasting pasta dish for any occasion.

Serves 2 | 550 calories per portion | 16g fat per portion

150g dried pappardelle
50g petit pois
12 asparagus tips (see Tip)
200g salmon fillet
50ml dry white wine
1 large or 2 small shallots, grated
1 tsp saffron threads in 2 tbsp hot vegetable stock
salt and black pepper
100g fromage frais, 8% fat
fresh dill, to garnish (optional)

1 Bring a large pan of salted water to the boil, add the pappardelle and cook for 10 minutes, or according to the pack instructions.

2 Halfway through the pasta cooking time, put the peas and asparagus on a steamer rack and steam over the pasta for 4 minutes or until just tender.

3 Meanwhile, put the salmon on a plate and microwave on medium-high for 4 minutes or poach gently in simmering water for 4 minutes until just cooked through; flake the fish and reserve.

4 While the pasta, vegetables and salmon are cooking, heat a non-stick frying pan, add the wine, shallots, saffron and stock mixture, and some seasoning and boil for a few minutes until the shallots have softened.

5 Reduce the heat to very low and stir in the fromage frais and combine well. Stir in the peas, asparagus and salmon flakes.

6 When the pasta is cooked, drain and return it to the pan with the contents of the frying pan, toss well to combine and serve garnished with a little dill, if you like.

serving suggestion Serve with a green salad.

tip You can use broad beans or artichoke hearts instead of the asparagus; if you use canned artichoke hearts, they won't need more than a minute's steaming to heat through.

fettucine with broad beans and prosciutto

Serves 2 | 460 calories per portion | 13.5g fat per portion

150g dried fettucine (see Tip)

175g shelled weight
baby broad beans

cooking oil spray

6 slices prosciutto (Parma ham)

1 tbsp olive oil

juice of ½ lemon

1 dsp chopped fresh mint

1 dsp chopped fresh parsley

salt and black pepper

1 tbsp grated Parmesan cheese,
to serve

1 Bring a large pan of salted water to the boil, add the
fettucine and cook for 6–8 minutes or according to the
pack instructions. Put a steamer rack on top of the pasta
and steam the broad beans for about 5 minutes, while the
pasta cooks. Remove the beans and set aside.

2 Meanwhile, spray a non-stick frying pan with the cooking
oil and add the ham slices. Cook over a medium-high
heat until golden, remove from the pan and allow to cool
for 1 minute, then crumble roughly in your fingers and
return to the frying pan.

3 Add the olive oil, drained beans, lemon juice, herbs and
seasoning to the pan and stir over a medium heat for
1–2 minutes.

4 By now the pasta should be cooked, so drain and return
it to the pan with the ham and bean mixture, toss well to
combine, then ladle into serving dishes and sprinkle with
the Parmesan cheese.

serving suggestion Serve with a simple herb salad.

tip Use spaghetti instead of fettucine in this dish, if preferred.

mediterranean baked chicken and rice

This is a really moreish dish, which no one will believe is low in fat.

Serves 4 | 505 calories per portion | 10g fat per portion

1½ tbsp olive oil

4 skinless chicken breast fillets, halved

1 large mild onion, thinly sliced

2 red peppers, deseeded and thinly sliced

2 cloves garlic, crushed

1 orange, peeled and segmented

8 black stoned olives, halved

dash of Tabasco

6 sun-dried tomatoes, finely chopped

1 tbsp tomato purée

1 tsp dried herbes de Provence or 1 tbsp mixed chopped fresh herbs (see Tip)

salt and black pepper

225g long-grain rice (see Tip)

400ml chicken stock

1 Heat half the oil in a flameproof casserole (see Tip) and sauté the chicken over a high heat, turning halfway through, for about 3 minutes until browned. Remove with a slotted spoon and reserve.

2 Add the rest of the oil and the onion and peppers, and sauté over a medium-high heat for 5 minutes until softened and turning slightly golden. Add the garlic for the last minute of cooking.

3 Add the orange, olives, Tabasco, sun-dried tomatoes, tomato purée, herbs and seasoning, and stir well, then add the rice and stir again.

4 Pour in the stock, bring to a simmer, then cover and transfer to a preheated oven, 170°C/337°F/Gas 3½, for 45–50 minutes until the chicken and rice are cooked and the stock is nearly completely absorbed. (Check about 10 minutes before the end of cooking time that there is still enough moisture left in the casserole. If not, add a little more hot stock or water.)

serving suggestion A green salad or green beans are good with this dish.

tips You can use parsley, basil, thyme, rosemary and oregano in this dish. If using rosemary, chop it very finely.

You can use brown rice or wholewheat grains, if preferred, in which case add another 20 minutes to the cooking time.

If you don't have a flameproof casserole, cook everything in a large non-stick frying pan up to step 4, then transfer the contents of the pan to a lidded casserole dish.

jambalaya

This Caribbean dish is hot and spicy and makes a good warm buffet dish.

Serves 4 | 520 calories per portion | 18g fat per portion

1½ tbsp olive oil

1 large Spanish onion, finely chopped

2 medium sticks celery, chopped

1 red pepper, deseeded and chopped

2 cloves garlic, crushed

300g monkfish fillet, cubed (see Tip)

100g chorizo sausage, sliced

225g long-grain rice

1 tsp turmeric

1 tsp chili powder (see Tip)

salt and black pepper

1 tbsp sun-dried tomato paste

1 tsp fresh thyme

500ml chicken stock

175g peeled prawns

25g shelled pistachio nuts

1 Heat the oil in a large, lidded non-stick frying pan and sauté the onion, celery and pepper over a medium heat for 5 minutes until softened, then add the garlic and stir for 1–2 minutes.

2 Add the monkfish, chorizo, rice, turmeric, chili powder, seasoning, tomato paste and thyme, stir well, then pour in the stock and bring to the boil.

3 Reduce the heat, stir, cover and simmer gently for 20 minutes or until the rice is tender. (If the rice isn't cooked and the liquid has been absorbed, add a little more hot stock or water and continue cooking for a few minutes.)

4 Stir in the prawns and nuts and cook for another 1–2 minutes to heat through.

serving suggestion This is a complete meal, but you could serve it with a plain green salad.

tips You can use swordfish instead of the monkfish.

Chili powder (one 'l' not two, as in chilli) is a Mexican-type spice mixture – if you can't find it, use any hot and spicy Caribbean or Mexican mixture.

pasta primavera

This dish is best served in late spring or early summer when the vegetables are in season and fresh.

Serves 2 | 410 calories per portion | 10.5g fat per portion

150g dried rigatoni

1 tbsp olive oil

2 medium shallots, very finely chopped

1 medium leek, very thinly sliced into rounds

1 medium carrot, sliced lengthways into wafer-thin slices

1 medium courgette, sliced lengthways into wafer-thin slices (see Tip)

50g very young and tender mangetout (see Tip)

1 clove fresh garlic, crushed

2 fresh ripe medium tomatoes, deseeded and roughly chopped

salt and black pepper

2 tbsp half-fat crème fraîche

fresh basil leaves, to garnish

1 Bring a large pan of salted water to the boil, add the pasta and cook for 10 minutes, or according to the pack instructions.

2 Meanwhile, heat the oil in a large non-stick frying pan and sauté the shallots, leek, carrot, courgette, mangetout and garlic over a medium-high heat for 5 minutes, adding a little water if the vegetables dry out.

3 Add the tomatoes to the frying pan with their juices and some seasoning. Stir, bring to a simmer and cook for 4 minutes over a medium-low heat, stirring from time to time.

4 When the pasta is cooked, drain and return it to the pan with the crème fraîche and vegetable mixture. Check the seasoning, toss well to combine and serve garnished with the basil.

serving suggestion This is a complete meal but you can add 1 tablespoon of grated Parmesan cheese to the finished dish, which would add 22 calories and about 1.5g fat per portion.

tips You can use asparagus or broccoli instead of the courgette.

Petit pois or baby broad beans can be substituted for the mangetout.

♡ spaghetti with spinach and ricotta

Serves 2 | 455 calories per portion | 18.5g fat per portion

150g dried spaghetti

2 fresh cloves garlic, peeled

sea salt

1 tbsp good quality olive oil

1 dsp balsamic vinegar

100g baby spinach leaves

75g ricotta cheese

20g pinenuts, toasted
(see Tip, page 93)

1 Bring a large pan of salted water to the boil, add the pasta and cook for 10 minutes, or according to the pack instructions.

2 Meanwhile, pound the garlic with a little sea salt in a pestle and mortar, then add the oil, mix again, and finally the vinegar.

3 When the pasta is cooked, drain, reserving 1 tablespoon or so of the cooking water. Return the pasta and reserved water to the saucepan and over a very low heat, toss it with the garlic and oil mixture. Add the baby spinach leaves and toss for 1–2 minutes until wilted.

4 Stir the ricotta into the pasta mixture to heat through, then ladle into serving bowls and sprinkle the toasted pinenuts over the top.

pasta, rice and grains

ᵛ pasta with garlic mushrooms

Serves 2 | 400 calories per portion | 13.5g fat per portion

150g dried macaroni or farfalle

1 tbsp olive oil

4 spring onions, chopped

100g fresh porcini mushrooms, sliced (see Tip)

4 large cloves garlic, crushed

25ml vegetable stock

salt and black pepper

1 tbsp chopped walnuts

1 tbsp chopped fresh flat-leaf parsley, plus a little extra to garnish

2 tbsp fromage frais, 8% fat (see Tip)

1 Bring a large pan of salted water to the boil, add the pasta and cook for 10 minutes, or according to the pack instructions.

2 Meanwhile, heat the oil in a non-stick frying pan and stir-fry the spring onions over a medium heat for 2 minutes, then add the mushrooms and garlic and stir-fry for another minute.

3 Add the stock and stir for a further minute, then add the seasoning, walnuts and parsley, reduce the heat and stir in the fromage frais. Stir well and heat through – take the pan off the heat if it is still too hot as you don't want the fromage frais to boil.

4 When the pasta is cooked, drain and return it to the pan with the contents of the frying pan. Toss well to combine and serve garnished with some extra parsley.

serving suggestion Serve with a herb salad.

tips If you can't get porcini mushrooms (sometimes called ceps), use chestnut or portobello mushrooms.

You could use 2 tablespoons of low-fat soft cheese instead of the fromage frais for a similar calorie and fat count.

salads

Salads and slimming would seem to go hand-in-hand – the ultimate cliché for weight watchers is the lettuce and cottage cheese lunch. However, a salad is not necessarily a low-fat feast at all. Many of the most famous salads from around the world, Caesar Salad or Coronation Chicken, for example, are higher in fat than many hot main courses. Additionally, most ready-to-eat salads bought from supermarkets are high-fat, high-calorie little dishes.

Yet you don't have to stick to that lettuce and cottage cheese lunch if you want to eat in a low-fat zone. All the revamped traditional salads in this chapter offer truly healthy, low-fat eating, while still bringing you all the taste, crunch, smoothness, creaminess (or whatever) of the originals.

You'll find reduced-fat versions of the above favourites as well as Italian Roast Pepper and Mozzarella Salad, Greek Salad with Feta, English Egg and Bacon Salad and French Salad Niçoise, plus plenty more tempting ideas – you need no longer suffer at the hands of the limp lettuce leaf.

There are also plenty of fresh and light salads that have become more familiar in recent years: Thai Beef Salad and Thai Pork and Noodle Salad, for example.

The main key to a low-fat salad is a low-fat dressing, but it must not be bland. I've made full use of fruit juices, vinegars, herbs, spices, soy and so on to add plenty of flavour. You'll also find more ideas for basic salad dressings and dips in the Dressings, Sauces and Stocks chapter (page 119).

Many of these salads make ideal starters in half or even quarter portions and all make great lunch or supper dishes.

broad bean, mozzarella and sun-dried tomato salad

A clean-tasting salad for a light lunch or supper.

Serves 4 | 175 calories per portion | 11g fat per portion

250g broad beans (see Tip)

salt

40g rocket leaves

50g baby spinach leaves

40g lamb's lettuce

40g sun-dried tomatoes, chopped (see Tip)

1 quantity Reduced-fat Vinaigrette (see page 120)

150g half-fat mozzarella cheese, roughly chopped

1 dsp each of chopped fresh mint and chives, to garnish

1 Cook the beans in boiling salted water for 4 minutes or until tender, then drain.

2 Combine the beans with the salad leaves, sun-dried tomatoes and the dressing, and arrange on four salad plates.

3 Sprinkle the mozzarella over the vegetables and garnish with the fresh herbs to serve.

serving suggestion Olive bread is good with this salad.

tips Use small and tender young broad beans, either fresh or frozen. Otherwise, if you have to use older ones, pop them out of their outer shells and just blanch the tender bright green beans.

Try to use sun-dried tomatoes packed in a vacuum pack or dry-packed in a bag as they contain virtually no fat, whereas those packed in oil in jars are high in both calories and fat.

pasta salad with tomatoes and pesto

This is one of my favourite summer salads, which is good as part of a buffet or you could add some chicken slices to make a more substantial meal.

Serves 4 | 370 calories per portion | 14g fat per portion

250g dried farfalle pasta (see Tip)

salt

2 cloves garlic, crushed

1 tbsp ready-made fresh basil pesto dressing (see Tip)

1 quantity Reduced-fat Vinaigrette (see page 120 and Tip)

200g cherry tomatoes, halved

1 tbsp dry packed, sun-dried tomatoes, finely chopped

12 black stoned olives, halved

bunch of spring onions, chopped

½ bunch of fresh basil

25g pinenuts, toasted, to serve (see Tip, page 93)

1 Cook the pasta in boiling salted water for 8 minutes or until just tender, drain and cool to room temperature.

2 Pound the garlic with the pesto dressing until well combined, then mix thoroughly with the vinaigrette.

3 Toss the pasta, cherry tomatoes, sun-dried tomatoes, olives and spring onions with the dressing. Stir in the basil leaves and sprinkle the pinenuts over to serve.

tips Farfalle are small bow-shaped shapes, but you could also use pasta shells.

Don't buy long-life pesto; get a good quality chilled variety, which you'll find in supermarkets.

Use 1 tablespoon of tomato juice instead of the grape juice in the dressing.

salads

mushroom and flageolet salad

Serves 4 | 135 calories per portion | 8.9g fat per portion

75g fine French beans, halved

salt

1 quantity Marinated Garlic Mushrooms (see page 21)

½ quantity Reduced-fat Vinaigrette (see page 120)

100g canned piquillo peppers (drained weight), chopped

75g canned flageolet beans (drained weight), rinsed (see Tip)

75g red chard leaves

1 tbsp chopped fresh flat-leaf parsley, to garnish

1 Blanch the French beans in lightly salted boiling water for 2 minutes or until barely tender (or steam for 2 minutes); drain.

2 Remove the mushrooms from the marinade with a slotted spoon and reserve.

3 Mix 2 tablespoons of the marinade with the vinaigrette and toss all the salad ingredients, except the parsley, in the dressing.

4 Serve with the parsley sprinkled on top.

tip You can use borlotti, cannellini or red kidney beans, if preferred.

ⓥ roast pepper and mozzarella salad

Serves 4 | 295 calories per portion | 14g fat per portion

2 red peppers, deseeded and each cut into 6 pieces

2 yellow peppers, deseeded and each cut into 6 pieces

1 medium aubergine, cut into 1cm thick rounds

6 good cloves garlic, left whole and unpeeled

1½ tbsp olive oil

salt and black pepper

125g dried penne pasta

1 quantity Reduced-fat Vinaigrette (see page 120)

100g half-fat mozzarella cheese, roughly chopped (see Tip)

1 Toss all the vegetables and garlic in the oil with plenty of seasoning. Arrange on a baking tray and roast in a preheated oven, 200°C/400°F/Gas 6, for 30–40 minutes until golden and tender.

2 Meanwhile, cook the pasta in boiling salted water for 10 minutes or until tender, then drain.

3 When the vegetables are cooked, remove the garlic cloves and press out the soft centres into the dressing. Beat well to combine.

4 Toss the still-warm vegetables with the pasta and dressing, and stir in the cheese before serving.

tip Use the soft, half-fat mozzarella that comes in a ball, packaged in brine; drain and rinse well before using. You can also use halloumi, ricotta or even feta instead of the mozzarella.

salads

greek salad with feta

Serves 4 | 220 calories per portion | 17g fat per portion

salads

100g cos lettuce, chopped

1 beef tomato, roughly chopped (see Tip)

¼ cucumber, roughly chopped

1 small red onion, very thinly sliced, then separated into rounds

1 yellow pepper, deseeded and roughly chopped

1 quantity Reduced-fat Vinaigrette (see page 120 and Tip)

200g Greek feta cheese

12 black stoned olives (see Tip)

1 handful fresh flat-leaf parsley, to garnish

1 Combine all the vegetables and stir in the dressing.

2 Arrange the salad on four serving plates and crumble over the feta cheese.

3 Top with the olives and garnish with parsley to serve.

serving suggestion Serve with chunks of rustic bread.

tips Pour any juice that escapes when you are cutting the tomato into the salad dressing.

Use 1 tablespoon of lemon juice instead of the grape juice in the dressing.

Try to get Greek Kalamata olives for this salad – they are small and very tasty, and available in jars in most supermarkets.

chicken caesar salad

Caesar salad is normally extremely high in fat but this version retains the spirit of the dish, while being quite light.

Serves 4 | 320 calories per portion | 15g fat per portion

125g ciabatta bread, cut into rough croûtons

300g cos lettuce, leaves torn into pieces

¼ cucumber (about 100g), deseeded and diced

300g smoked chicken breast, cut into slices (see Tip)

4 rinsed and dried anchovies, chopped

25g Parmesan cheese, shaved

FOR THE DRESSING

1 large soft-boiled egg, shelled (see Tip)

2 tbsp low-fat natural bio yogurt

1 tbsp olive oil

1 dsp balsamic vinegar

2 tsp Dijon mustard

1 clove garlic, crushed

dash of Worcestershire sauce

salt and black pepper

1 Bake the croûtons in a preheated oven, 200°C/400°F/Gas 6, for 10 minutes or until they are golden; reserve.

2 Blend all the dressing ingredients together in an electric blender (see Tip).

3 Toss the lettuce, cucumber and chicken with the dressing, and arrange on serving plates.

4 Scatter over the chopped anchovies and the shavings of Parmesan to serve.

salads

tips You can use ordinary cooked chicken, if preferred.

If you don't have a suitable electric blender, simply beat all the dressing ingredients together thoroughly in a mixing bowl using a wooden spoon so that the egg breaks down and combines thoroughly.

This recipe contains partly cooked eggs. If you put the egg into boiling water, it should be ready in about 3 minutes; remove with a slotted spoon and cool under running water for a few minutes to stop it cooking further, then shell it.

thai pork and noodle salad

Serves 4 | 300 calories per portion | 8g fat per portion

1 tbsp groundnut oil

400g pork tenderloin, cut into
0.5cm thick slices (see Tip)

1 dsp fresh grated ginger

150g dried udon noodles

½ quantity Thai Dressing
(see page 122)

50g fresh beansprouts

100g pak choi

handful of fresh basil, to garnish

1 Heat the oil in a non-stick frying pan and stir-fry the pork over a high heat for 2–3 minutes or until browned and cooked through. Add the ginger and stir-fry for 30 seconds.

2 Boil the noodles according to the pack instructions, then drain.

3 Make up the dressing, if necessary, and toss it with the pork, noodles, beansprouts and pak choi.

4 Serve the salad, garnished with basil.

tip You can use chicken fillet instead of the pork for a similar calorie and fat count.

thai beef salad

A luxurious hot and spicy salad, which is ideal for a winter's lunch.

Serves 4 | 170 calories per portion | 5g fat per portion

cooking oil spray

black pepper

400g fillet of beef in a single joint

½ cucumber (about 200g), halved lengthways, deseeded and cut into thin strips (see Tip)

1 romaine or cos lettuce, leaves roughly torn

50g red mustard leaf or watercress, thinly sliced

40g hot radishes, very thinly sliced

100g fresh beansprouts

handful of fresh basil, to garnish

FOR THE DRESSING

2 cloves garlic, peeled

4 tbsp Thai Dressing (see page 122)

handful each of fresh coriander and basil

salt and black pepper

1 Heat a griddle or non-stick frying pan or grill, and spray with cooking oil. Grind some black pepper all over the beef and sear it on all sides until well browned (see Tip). Set aside, cover and leave to cool.

2 Meanwhile, make the dressing. Pound the garlic (preferably using a pestle and mortar) with a little of the dressing, then add the coriander and basil and the rest of the dressing and pound again thoroughly to combine. (As the Thai Dressing is quite salty you may not need any extra salt.) Check seasoning.

3 Thinly slice the beef, which will still be very pink in the middle.

4 Toss the vegetables and beef with the dressing and garnish with basil leaves.

tips Try to get an organic cucumber, which is much tastier and less watery.

When you cook the beef, leave it completely alone for at least 2 minutes so that it seals, otherwise it may stick when you try to move it. Repeat this four times, each time turning the beef by a quarter, so that it browns evenly. Keep the heat as high as you can.

salads

salmon and avocado salad

Most of the fat in this salad is the 'good for you' omega-3 fatty acids or healthy monounsaturated oil.

Serves 4 | 270 calories per portion | 18g fat per portion

350g salmon fillets

16 asparagus tips

1 small head oak leaf lettuce (about 100g)

50g baby red chard or baby spinach leaves

handful of watercress

½ small ripe avocado, peeled, stoned and sliced

8 spring onions, finely chopped, to garnish

FOR THE DRESSING

2 tbsp half-fat crème fraîche (see Tip)

2–3 tbsp skimmed milk

½ small ripe avocado, peeled, stoned and roughly chopped

few sprigs of watercress

1 tsp lemon juice

pinch of caster sugar

salt and black pepper

1 Microwave the salmon on a medium-high heat for 3 minutes, or poach it, until just cooked, then flake (keeping the flakes large, if possible).

2 Steam the asparagus for about 5 minutes until just tender, then refresh under cold running water, pat dry and reserve.

3 Blend all the dressing ingredients together in an electric blender and check the seasoning, adding a little more skimmed milk, if necessary, to make a good pouring sauce.

4 Arrange the lettuce, chard or spinach, watercress, salmon, asparagus and avocado on serving plates and drizzle the dressing over, then garnish with the spring onions.

serving suggestion Brown bread is all you need with this salad.

tip You can use 8% fat fromage frais instead of the crème fraîche, for a slightly creamier, milder tasting dressing. The calorie and fat count will be almost the same.

desserts and bakes

Desserts, puddings and bakes are usually the first meals and treats to go when we are trying to eat less fat and it is true that many are too high in fat to fit comfortably into a healthy eating regime. Yet it is a shame if you do discard them, as they have a lot to offer nutritionally. Many are dairy-based, which is a good source of calcium, often a shortfall in our diets; others are a good source of fibre, vitamins and minerals.

Of course, fresh fruit makes a perfectly satisfactory ending to a meal but now and then everyone needs something a bit different and all fruits can be transformed into the most glorious, tantalising, yet low-fat, puddings and desserts. Bakes also need not be high calorie and unhealthy. My recipes make full use of low-fat dairy produce, wholegrains, fresh and dried fruits, and fat-free ingredients to bring you tasty treats suitable for any occasion. All are suitable for vegetarians, except those using gelatine, in which case agar agar can be used instead.

Even if you don't feel like anything more than basic cooking, there are plenty of quick, healthy ideas for sweet treats that you can try. Grill or bake your fruit instead of eating it raw – bananas grilled in their skins, opened and drizzled with orange juice or low-fat chocolate sauce are lovely, or try strawberries marinated in balsamic vinegar, or baked apples or peaches. Poached dried fruits make a good winter dessert, or you can make a quick summer pudding by poaching summer berries, then soaking pieces of bread in the ruby red juice.

For something quick, creamy and indulgent, try puréed or stewed fruit mixed with low-fat fromage frais and icing sugar, or ready-made meringues crumbled and stirred into Greek yogurt with raspberries. Why? Because you deserve it!

ginger plum custard

A warming, easy family pudding for an autumn evening.

Serves 4 | 225 calories per portion | 5g fat per portion

450g red ripe dessert plums, halved and stoned (see Tip)

75g caster sugar

2cm piece of stem ginger, finely chopped

2 large free-range eggs

300ml semi-skimmed milk

½ tsp vanilla extract

1 dsp stem ginger syrup

40ml honey

1 Arrange the plums skin-side up in a shallow ovenproof dish, then sprinkle with a third of the sugar and the stem ginger.

2 Whisk the eggs with the remaining sugar until creamy, then beat in the milk and vanilla, and pour the mixture over the plums.

3 Put the dish in a roasting pan and pour boiling water in the tin to come halfway up the sides of the dish. Bake in a preheated oven, 150°C/300°F/Gas 2, for about 40 minutes or until lightly set.

4 Gently heat the ginger syrup and honey in a small saucepan and drizzle over the plum custard to serve.

tip You can make a similar fruit custard using tinned or fresh poached apricot halves, or baked rhubarb stems, or quartered and peeled ripe dessert pears.

℠ strawberry brûlée

A quick and easy version of the classic brûlée, which you will make time and again in the summer.

Serves 4 | 255 calories per portion | 10g fat per portion

250g strawberries, hulled and sliced (see Tip)

1 dsp icing sugar

1 vanilla pod

400ml Greek yogurt

100g caster sugar

1 Arrange the strawberries in the base of four ramekin dishes and sprinkle evenly with the icing sugar.

2 Scrape the seeds from the vanilla pod and stir into the yogurt, then spread the mixture evenly over the fruit in the ramekins and chill for 2 hours.

3 Preheat the grill to high. Sprinkle the caster sugar evenly over the top of the yogurt so that it is well covered.

4 Place the ramekins on a baking tray and flash under the grill – near the heat – for a few minutes until the sugar has melted and is golden and bubbling (see Tip). Remove and serve (the top will set almost straight away).

tips Fresh raspberries, ripe peeled peaches or lightly poached blueberries or blackberries can be substituted for the strawberries. Avoid adding too much liquid with the fruit, as it will spoil the brûlée.

You can use a blow torch to caramelise the sugar – they are obtainable from cookshops or by mail order, starting from around £15.00.

desserts and bakes

blackcurrant cheesecake

Cheesecake is one of those desserts which fat and calorie watchers always, sadly, try to avoid, so it is marvellous to be able to include this one in your eating plan now and again.

Serves 6 | 245 calories per portion | 12g fat per portion

200g Greek yogurt
150g low-fat soft cheese
150g fromage frais, 8% fat
30g fructose
10g sachet gelatine
3 tbsp hot water

FOR THE BASE

45g low-fat spread
2 tbsp pear and apple spread (see Tip)
25g wholemeal breadcrumbs
25g rolled oats
25g wholemeal flour
20g ground almonds

FOR THE TOPPING

200g blackcurrants (see Tip)
2 tbsp water
20g fructose
1 rounded tsp arrowroot

1 To make the base, warm the low-fat spread with the pear and apple spread in a mixing bowl for a few seconds in the microwave until runny. Stir together, then add the rest of the ingredients for the base to the bowl and mix thoroughly.

2 Press the base mixture into the bottom of a 20cm non-stick, springform flan tin and bake in a preheated oven, 190°C/375°F/Gas 5, for 12 minutes, then remove and leave to cool.

3 Meanwhile, make the cheesecake. Mix together the yogurt, soft cheese, fromage frais and the 30g fructose in a mixing bowl.

4 Sprinkle the gelatine over the hot water in a small bowl and leave for 5 minutes, then finish dissolving it over a pan of just-boiled water. Stir 1 tablespoonful of the cheese mixture into the gelatine, then return this to the main cheese mixture and combine thoroughly.

5 Pour the cheesecake mixture on top of the base and chill for 5 hours.

6 For the topping, put the blackcurrants in a saucepan with the water and simmer for 10 minutes or until the juices are running and the blackcurrants are tender. Stir in the 20g fructose until dissolved.

7 Mix the arrowroot with a little cold water, stir into the blackcurrant mixture and simmer for 1 minute until the juice has thickened. Leave to cool, then spoon it over the top of the cheesecake to serve.

tips Several brands of pear and apple spread are widely sold in healthfood shops and delicatessens.

You can make the topping using a can or jar of black cherries – thickening a little of the juice in the same way as above.

♡ pears in rosé wine

A pretty way to serve pears in a rich and delicious sauce.

Serves 4 | 220 calories per portion | trace of fat per portion

½ bottle of rosé wine (see Tip)

150ml apple juice

1 sachet mulled wine spices (see Tip)

75g caster sugar

4 ripe but firm Comice pears, peeled, leaving the stalks attached (see Tip)

1 Put the wine and apple juice in a saucepan (see Tip) with the spice sachet and the sugar and warm over a medium heat, stirring, until the sugar dissolves.

2 Put the pears in the saucepan with the stalks uppermost. Add a little water to just about cover the pears.

3 Bring to the boil, then reduce the heat, cover and simmer, for 25 minutes or until the pears are tender – don't overcook them. Remove them from the pan and set aside to cool a little.

4 Return the pan to a high heat and boil, uncovered, for about 15 minutes or until the liquid has reduced to the consistency of a coating sauce (about 200ml).

5 Arrange the pears on a serving dish and pour the sauce over (see Tip).

serving suggestion Serve with a small dollop of half-fat crème fraîche.

tips Red wine is a good alternative to the rosé, although you may need to add a little extra sugar. You can also use all wine instead of part apple juice. Again, you will need an extra 25g sugar or thereabouts.

You can buy sachets of mulled wine spices from wine merchants or from most supermarkets.

Any variety of dessert pear will suffice, although Comice have a superb flavour.

Use a saucepan in which the pears fit tightly, so that they don't fall over. You also will not need too much extra liquid to cover them.

You can leave the pears in the poaching syrup for several hours, basting occasionally, to deepen the pinky red pigment in the pears.

desserts and bakes

bread and butter pudding

This is an interesting take on the traditional layered bread and butter pudding with only a tenth of the fat.

Serves 4 | 230 calories per portion | 5g fat per portion

50g sultanas

50g ready-to-eat dried apricots, chopped

150ml apple juice

20g butter

1 tsp mixed spice

125g slightly stale bread, cut into small cubes (see Tip)

1 large banana, chopped

150ml skimmed milk

1 tbsp golden caster sugar

1 Put the dried fruits, apple juice, butter and spice in a saucepan and stir over a medium heat until the butter has melted.

2 Add the bread and banana to the pan and stir well.

3 Tip the mixture into a shallow ovenproof dish and spread it out evenly. Pour the milk over everything and sprinkle with the sugar.

4 Bake in a preheated oven, 190°C/375°F/Gas 5, for 30 minutes until golden brown.

serving suggestion Half-fat custard or Greek yogurt are delicious with this pudding.

tip Brown or white bread is fine but it should be good quality. You could also use brioche, which would add just a few calories and 1g of fat per portion.

ⓥ chocolate chip muffins

A taste of chocolate is always a nice treat when you're watching your fat intake.

Makes 12 | 190 calories per portion | 4g fat per portion

300g plain flour

2 tsp baking powder

150g golden caster sugar

50g chocolate chips, milk or plain (see Tips)

1 large free-range egg

225ml skimmed milk

2 tbsp sunflower oil

1 tsp vanilla extract

1 Arrange 12 muffin cases in a 12-cup muffin tin.

2 Sift the flour and baking powder into a mixing bowl and stir in the sugar and chocolate chips.

3 In another bowl, combine the egg, milk, oil and vanilla, beating well.

4 Tip the milk mixture into a well in the flour mixture and mix together quickly – don't overmix or the muffins will become tough; you don't need a smooth mixture.

5 Spoon the mixture into the muffin cases and bake in a preheated oven, 200°C/400°F/Gas 6, for 15 minutes or until the muffins have risen and are golden and firm in the middle when lightly pressed with a finger. Cool on a rack and serve warm or cold (see Tip).

tips You can buy ready-prepared chocolate chips in small bags at the baking counter in supermarkets. For a little extra luxury, buy 50g good quality Belgian chocolate and chip it yourself – refrigerate or freeze it until very hard, put inside a plastic bag and crack with a rolling pin until you have small pieces.

You can use 100g fresh blueberries instead of the chocolate, which will save 16 calories and 1g fat per portion.

These muffins will keep for a day.

desserts and bakes

[ⓥ] banana bread

This is a moist teabread, which is as satisfying as a slice of cake but much lower in fat.

Makes 8 slices | 160 calories per portion | 4.5g fat per portion

100g self-raising flour
75g wholemeal self-raising flour
1 tsp baking powder
40g butter
50g soft dark brown sugar
1 level tsp mixed spice
60ml skimmed milk
2 ripe bananas, mashed

1 Grease and line a 450g (1lb) loaf tin with baking parchment (see Tip).

2 Sift the flours and baking powder into a mixing bowl, then rub in the butter until the mixture resembles fine breadcrumbs.

3 Stir in the sugar and spice, then stir in the milk and bananas, and mix well.

4 Spoon the mixture into the loaf tin and bake in a preheated oven, 180°C/350°F/Gas 4, for 40 minutes or until the loaf has risen and is golden and firm in the centre, and when a skewer inserted into the centre comes out clean.

5 Turn out and cool on a wire rack.

serving suggestion You can spread slices of banana bread with a little low-fat spread at 20 calories and 2g fat per teaspoon.

tip You can double the quantity of the mixture and cook in a 900g (2lb) loaf tin, or make double quantity in 2 × 450g (1lb) tins and freeze the second one.

dressings, sauces and stocks

Many hundreds of grams of fat and very many calories can be consumed in the form of salad dressings, dips, sauces for meats and fish, and so on. Yet I am not a great believer in making strange and complicated low-fat concoctions for salads – and similar – that aim to replace the high-fat versions, but which always seem to turn out a disappointment in both flavour and texture.

In general, the best idea is to choose sauces and dressings that are naturally low in fat, such as salsas, Thai-style dips and dressings, vegetable-based sauces, and spice mixtures, or creamy yogurt-based sauces like tzatziki or raita.

The selection of 'extras' in this chapter are all included because they are delicious in their own right, whether you are fat and calorie watching, or not. Even the Reduced-fat Vinaigrette and the Mayonnaise substitute, while not being quite as unctuous and wonderful as their full-fat versions, are nevertheless perfectly satisfactory, and both will save you masses of calories if you eat a lot of salad or are a compulsive mayonnaise-dipper.

I have also given a basic recipe for vegetable stock, as a good stock is easy to prepare and can make the difference between an excellent sauce, stew or soup and an indifferent one. Otherwise, use good quality ready-made chilled stock, or, in the case of vegetable stock, use Marigold bouillon, which is very acceptable and comes in a low-salt version.

If you don't want to make your own, Heidelberg make an acceptable range of low-fat dressings. There are many other low-fat brands on the market but few are really delicious.

reduced-fat vinaigrette

Makes enough to dress a salad for 4 people | 60 calories per portion | 6g fat per portion

2 tbsp extra-virgin olive oil
1 tbsp balsamic vinegar
1 tbsp red grape juice (see Tip)
1 tsp Dijon mustard (see Tip)
1 tsp caster sugar
salt and black pepper

1 Put all the ingredients in a screw-top jar and shake vigorously to combine.

2 Taste and adjust the seasoning as necessary (see Tip).

serving suggestion Use in the appropriate recipes in this book or for any salad that requires French dressing or vinaigrette.

tips You can use white grape juice, if preferred.

You can use either wholegrain Dijon mustard or the smooth type.

The dressing will keep for 1–2 weeks in the fridge.

[⊗] low-fat mayonnaise

Makes 4 tablespoons | 28.5 calories per portion | 2.5g fat per tablespoon

2 tbsp low-fat natural bio yogurt (see Tip)

1 tbsp reduced-fat, ready-made mayonnaise

1 dsp lemon juice (see Tip)

1 tsp smooth Dijon mustard

salt and black pepper

1 Beat together the yogurt and mayonnaise in a mixing bowl, using a wooden spoon.

2 Stir in the lemon juice, mustard and seasoning and stir again; check the seasoning.

3 Chill before serving (see Tip).

tips I always use bio yogurt because it has a mild and creamy flavour with no hint of sourness.

You can use lime juice instead of the lemon juice, and add 1 teaspoon of Thai fish sauce (nam pla) for a slightly spicy sauce to go with grilled prawns or salmon.

This will keep for 1–2 days, covered, in the fridge.

dressings, sauces and stocks

thai dressing

Makes 8 tablespoons | 10.5 calories per portion | negligible fat per tablespoon

2 tbsp rice vinegar

2 tbsp lime juice

1½ tbsp Thai fish sauce (nam pla)

1 tbsp caster sugar

1 clove garlic, crushed

1 hot red chilli, deseeded and very finely chopped (see Tip)

1 Put all the ingredients in a screw-top jar and shake vigorously to combine.

2 Leave for several hours, shaking once or twice, so that the sugar has thoroughly dissolved and the flavours have time to mingle.

serving suggestion This is good on any Thai-style meat or fish salad and you can also use it on a plain salad to serve with grilled or roast meat or crabcakes (see page 86).

tip If you want a really hot dressing, you can leave the chilli seeds in.

℗ dry spice mix

Makes about 7 tablespoons | 10 calories per portion | trace of fat per tablespoon

3 tbsp ground turmeric

2 tbsp ground coriander seeds

1 dsp ground cumin seeds

1 tsp each of ground cardamom seeds, chilli, cloves, ginger and black pepper

Combine all the spices together in a mixing bowl. Transfer to a lidded container and store in a cool, dark, dry place (see Tips). Use as directed in the Quick Vegetable Curry recipe (see page 89) or in your own curries, soups and casseroles.

tips It is best to buy spices whole and grind them yourself, particularly coriander, cumin and black pepper. Ground spices quickly lose their flavour.

A good way to grind spices is in a coffee grinder, kept especially for the purpose. A pestle and mortar will crush spices but not as thoroughly as a grinder.

The spice mix will keep for a few weeks before losing its flavour and aroma.

ⓥ basic vegetable stock

Makes 1 litre | negligible calories

1 onion, chopped

2 carrots, chopped

1 leek, chopped

2 sticks celery, chopped

1 bouquet garni

several black peppercorns

salt

1 litre water

1 Put all the ingredients in a lidded saucepan and bring to the boil.

2 Skim off any foam that forms on the top, reduce the heat and simmer for 30 minutes.

3 Allow to cool a little, strain through a sieve and cool. Discard the vegetables and use the stock within 24 hours or freeze.

chicken stock

about 60 calories | 5g fat for the whole quantity

Add a whole uncooked chicken carcass to the recipe above and cook for 2 hours, then cool and strain. When cold, skim any fat off the surface and use as directed in the recipe.

fish stock

about 30 calories | 1g fat for the whole quantity

Follow the basic vegetable stock recipe but omit the carrots and leek and add 1kg raw fish bones and trimmings to the water. Simmer for 30 minutes, strain and cool.

meat stock

about 60 calories | 5g fat for the whole quantity

Follow the basic vegetable stock recipe but add 500g raw red meat bones and lean trimmings to the water. Cook for 3 hours, strain and cool, then skim any fat off the surface.

tips Roast the bones and meat trimmings in a preheated oven, 180°C/350°F/Gas 4, for 1 hour before adding to the water for extra flavour.

Once the stock is strained, cooled and skimmed of fat, as necessary, you can increase its flavour. Tip the stock into a saucepan and boil rapidly until reduced – the more you reduce it, the stronger it will become.

**To order your copy
of Judith Wills'**

TOP 200
LOW FAT
RECIPES

at the special price of £16.99 (normal rrp £18.99)

published by Headline please send a cheque payable

to BOOKSHOP PARTNERSHIP LTD to Top 200 Offer,

Dept BSH135, PO BOX 104, Ludlow SY8 1YB or call

08707552122 and quote the reference BSH135.

6 WAYS TO LOSE A STONE IN 6 WEEKS

JUDITH WILLS

Somehow you've put on a surplus stone and you know you could lose it if only you could find the right diet.

Here are six to choose from – and one of them's bound to be just right for you:

The Detox and Energise Plan

The Fast Food Plan

The Sweet-Tooth Plan

The Meat-Free Plan

The Business Plan

The Family Plan

These are easy-to-follow regimes with masses of helpful tips and straightforward instructions on how to improve your eating habits, pep up your body with a little exercise and keep the weight off permanently.

Judith Wills is one of Britain's best-known slimming and nutrition experts. Former editor of *Slimmer* magazine, she has also made three bestselling videos and is an acclaimed cookery writer.

'A book that would give even the most hesitant dieter confidence' *Healthy Eating*

NON-FICTION / DIET 0 7472 6423 6

THE OMEGA DIET

JUDITH WILLS

Good to eat, good for you and good for
your weight

The Omega Diet

- Is the most natural way to lose pounds
and eat well

- Tells you how to get slim and feel great on just
twelve different units of food a day

- Contains all the nutrients and calories you need
for optimum health without calorie counting, label
reading, weighing and measuring

The Omega Diet tells you

- Why low-fat, no-fat diets are bad for you and
may be bad for your weight

- Which foods are best for your body and for
weight control

- How to lose up to 7lb in 14 days on the
Omega system – and keep it off

- Just how simple a truly healthy diet can be

The Omega Diet is as near nutritionally perfect
a diet as you can get

NON-FICTION / HEALTH 0 7472 6480 5